Newbies

by William Edwards MBCS

Version 1.1
Updated: 2017

KINDLE EDITION

Statement of Rights

The Newbies Books

This volume is a Boxed Set of Newbies Books 1-3, put together as a handy, single reference for anyone studying for the ITIL® Foundation Examination or simply wanting to learn more about the IT Service Management discipline.

At present there are three books in this series, with more to follow. Although they can be read in any order, if you are new to the subject of IT Service Management, it is best to read them in the order they are presented in this work.

The ebook versions can also be obtained individually ...

> IT Service Management for Newbies (Book #1)
>
> Incident Management for Newbies (Book #2)
>
> Problem Management for Newbies (Book #3)

Please Note: in the interests of readability, the glossary of terms, which appears in each of the above books, has been included just once, at the end of this combined volume. Similarly, the Contents pages have been combined to form a single Table of Contents.

Table of Contents

Part 1

IT Service Management for Newbies

Foreword to IT Service Management

When I first encountered ITIL®, I had already been working within the IT industry for many years. I was Technical Manager at Apricot Computers in the UK. I am a graduate of the University of Birmingham (in the UK) and a lifetime member of the British Computing Society. I mention these facts because, despite my background, my professional qualifications and my extensive practical experience within the computing industry, I struggled with ITIL® at the beginning.

It is not that any of this stuff is difficult - it really is not – however, the source material, as you will know if you have looked at it, is certainly not too accessible to beginners. That's because it is not meant to be introductory material. It is, of course, reference material. In addition, the source books are written by people who understand the discipline very well and are fluent in the management-speak of their peers. There is nothing wrong with any of that, except that beginners often do not possess the necessary specialist vocabulary to be able to understand it.

At the time, I turned to Amazon to look for a good introductory text on the subject and, although I bought all of the source material – quite an investment as you may know - and a number of additional books on the subject, I was eventually forced to conclude that there simply were no good quality introductory texts available at the time.

So I leaned about Service Management the hard way; by working hard, studying the books and passing the exams. I became qualified as a Service Manager – what was often referred to as the 'Red Badge' qualification back in the early days of ITIL® - and then went on to pass *all* of the present exams in the new qualification program. Yes, every single exam, not just those you need to pass to achieve the new *ITIL Expert* qualification which, of course, I do also hold.

For the past 13 years, I have been consulting, teaching and helping people to implement Service Management based on ITIL® best practice guidance and this book, the result of years of study, reflection and application of the principles, represents my contribution to the online knowledgebase. If you are new to the subject of ITIL® and Service Management and you want to learn what it is all about, then this book was written for you.

Introduction to IT Service Management

Let's start by talking about what Service Management actually is, and then we can move on and look at the subject of IT Service Management.

Service Management was started outside of the IT arena by organisations like banks and airlines that wanted to improve their customer experience. Basically, they were looking for ways to provide better quality services and they wanted to operate more efficiently. The result was the birth of Service Management as a discipline.

The ITIL® books attempt to document the application of Service Management principles to the IT world. It is a UK government initiative and it seeks to draw from various good practices commonly operating in the real world and distil what is referred to as *Best Practice* from those real-world methods.

This Best Practice guidance is documented in a series of publications produced by the Office of Government Commerce – the OGC.

Here is a list of the Official ITIL® publications:

ITIL® Core Guidance - Print Versions
ISBN 9780113313044 Service Strategy (SS)

ISBN 9780113313051 Service Design (SD)
ISBN 9780113313068 Service Transition (ST)
ISBN 9780113313075 Service Operation (SO)
ISBN 9780113313082 Continual Service Improvement
(CSI)

You can also get them as eBook versions (the wonders of
modern technology eh?) ...

ITIL® Core Guidance - eBook Versions
ISBN 9780113313105 Service Strategy (SS)
ISBN 9780113313112 Service Design (SD)
ISBN 9780113313129 Service Transition (ST)
ISBN 9780113313136 Service Operation (SO)
ISBN 9780113313143 Continual Service Improvement
(CSI)

Tip – You can often get reused print versions on eBay at a
fraction of the price of the new books!

Let's now take a quick look at some very common
misconceptions.

ITIL® is NOT ...

   - A Methodology
   - A Formal Standard
   - A Rigid System

People new to Service Management will often think that the ITIL® books might contain all the answers to the problems of managing an IT service operation. However, that is simply not the case and the books were never intended to be that.

They were not meant to be a methodology or a system or a formal standard – they are simply meant to provide GUIDANCE. That means that all the answers are definitely not in there. Nevertheless, the guidance is pretty comprehensive as we shall see and, whereas ITIL® is not a formal standard, it has come to be considered as the worldwide de-facto standard for IT Service Management.

The last thing we should briefly discuss, before getting into the nitty-gritty, is a little about the history of ITIL®. It began in the 1980s and the original books were published by the CCTA – Central Computing and Telecommunications Agency. The CCTA no longer exists as such. It was 'swallowed up' by the OGC (Office of Government Commerce).

There was a rewrite (mid 1990s – 2004) which led to Version 2 being released. The Version 2 Library (as it became popularly known) consisted of 9 Books. There were 7 subjects, but a couple of them were divided into parts 1 and 2. Later, the guidance was again rewritten and the resulting Version 3 guidance – consisting of just 5 publications in its core - was published in the summer of 2007.

In 2011, the Version 3 guidance was further revised. The changes were all minor. A couple of 'new' processes were added. I say 'new' because they were not named as processes previously, but they were already present in the V3 books. Other than that and a quick once over to correct mistakes, the most changed book was Service Strategy.

None of the concepts changed at all, but many people had struggled with the V3 Service Strategy volume. It needed an update and I am glad to see that it has now been completed. This new version of the guidance is now officially known as ITIL® 2011.

By the way the acronym originally stood for ...

- I ... Information
- T ... Technology
- I ... Infrastructure
- L ... Library

However, these days, it is regarded as unimportant what the letters stood for as the guidance is no longer regarded as a library. ITIL® is now simply considered by the cognoscenti as documented *Best Practice for IT Service Management*.

The De-Facto Standard

It was Version 2 of ITIL® that really took off!

Many public and private sector organisations that adopted IT Service Management made use of the V2 guidance. Other frameworks for Service Management, such as MOF (Microsoft Operations Framework) and the open source COBIT (Control Objectives for Information and Related Technology) basically lost the race.

This does not mean that MOF and COBIT are not useful and relevant; they certainly are and indeed ITIL® itself acknowledges their strengths. COBIT is stronger in audit and governance, for example. But, just as the VHS standard for video recorders prevailed rather than the technically superior Beetamax, so ITIL® eventually was hailed as the de-facto standard for IT Service Management.

Hey wait a minute – isn't this book about ITIL® 2011?

Yes: this book *is* about ITIL® 2011. But do you know something? All of the Version 2 processes continue to live in Version 3 and beyond, and Version 2 will be much easier for you to get your head around. So that makes it a very good place to start.

Version 2 was, very much, a process-based approach to the subject of IT Service Management, so before we can understand it, we need to understand what a **process** actually is, how it differs from a **function** and what are its characteristics.

OK, so here we go …

Functions and Processes

Here is the definition of a **process** taken from the official glossary:

A structured set of Activities designed to accomplish a specific Objective. A Process takes one or more defined inputs and turns them into defined outputs. A Process may include any of the Roles, responsibilities, tools and management Controls required to reliably deliver the outputs. A Process may define Policies, Standards, Guidelines, Activities, and Work Instructions if they are needed.

Does that kind of language leave you a bit cold?

Yes – well that's why you bought this book isn't it – so we could get away from that stuff and find out what it actually means. Here's my definition: if you were baking a cake, the **process** would be the recipe.

Now that's much better isn't it!

A recipe is not just a list of ingredients, but a whole series of tasks that need to be completed in order to turn the ingredients (inputs) into deliverables like cake (outputs); and that's what a process does. Processes have input(s) and output(s); they have a specific goal; and they have roles and responsibilities assigned to the individual tasks that transform those inputs into the outputs.

Now let's take a specific example: Incident Management –
that's a ***process*** and it involves people who work on the
Service Desk. By the way, the Service Desk is defined as a
function in ITIL®. A function (we'll be discussing a number
of them later on) consists of the people who actually carry
out processes.

So here we have a good working example of the
relationship between ***functions*** and **processes**: the Service
Desk function is involved in the Incident Management
process. A good way to think of it is that processes are
what is being done and functions are the people *who are
doing it*.

In ITIL® we have a *Service Desk* rather than a *Help Desk*:
after all, we are *Service Providers*, the discipline is known
as *Service Management*, so we have a *Service Desk*. Now
let's just think about what happens when someone calls
the *Service Desk*.

- We would start off by logging the call
- We would categorise and prioritise the call
- We would try to resolve the issue
- If unable to resolve, we would escalate
- The relevant specialist would resolve the issue
- We would keep track of things
- Eventually, the call would be closed

Later, we'll discuss each of those steps in more detail. But, for now, just recognise that a set of sequential activities are initiated when someone calls the Service desk and this is an excellent example of a *process.* The above list of activities are, essentially, the steps of the Incident Management *process* and, that process is performed by the Service Desk *function.*

There are other functions typically involved in the Incident Management process – that's what is meant by the phrase *functional escalation* - but more about them later. For now, we are concerned with simply understanding the difference between a process and a function.

To recap:

- Process: *what* is being done
- Function: *who* is doing it

There – that wasn't too bad was it?

The Incident Management process is one of 26 processes defined in the current version i.e. ITIL® 2011.

In the Version 2 foundation course, you would have studied only 10 processes - 5 processes were defined in the old Blue Book (Service Support) and a further 5 were defined in the old Red Book (Service Delivery). All 10 of the old V2 processes are present (with some slight renaming) in the present version.

Version 2 in Some Detail

This section is important to your understanding of ITIL®
2011 – I want you to understand that. Of course, there are
differences between V2 and subsequent versions but
(apart from process names) in this section, I have avoided
using V2 terms where they were not carried forward to
subsequent versions. This was a deliberate decision to
eliminate any possible confusion.

Because Version 2 contained less processes, I firmly
believe that a new student stands a far better chance of
understanding how they fit together and gaining that
holistic understanding of IT Service Management is very
important. But there is another excellent reason for
starting with Version 2 – in the real world, that is still what
many organisations effectively have in place.

Once we have looked at Version 2, we will go on to
consider how the structure of the guidance changed with
the introduction of subsequent versions.

So, let's make a start ...

Here is a list of the 10 processes that made up Version 2:

Service Support Processes

- Incident Management
- Problem Management

- Change Management
- Release Management
- Configuration Management

Service Delivery Processes

- Service Level Management
- Financial Management
- Capacity Management
- Availability Management
- IT Service Continuity Management (ITSCM)

Now then, what were all those processes about? Well let's start off with the old Red Book (Service Delivery) processes and take a look at each one in turn.

Service Level Management

The Service Level Management process seeks to document the requirements of the business – they are known as SLRs (Service Level Requirements).

In general, the business is not expected to understand the technical aspects of IT, so the requirements may not be well thought out or may even be downright unreasonable, however, this process (SLM) will engage in a negotiation to achieve an agreement with which everybody is happy. During those negotiations, we will reach a point where the business believes the proposed service levels will meet the business requirement and the IT staff believe the levels of service specified in the agreement can be met, working within the allocated budget.

The process of arriving at that agreement can be a lengthy one. It is often iterative, in that, once the business fully appreciates the financial implications of the initially presented requirements (SLRs), it may change those requirements. This is not weakness; it is just the reality of how negotiation works.

Eventually, an agreement is reached where the business will agree to what is to be subsequently provided, in terms of:

- Storage/throughput – known as *Capacity* in ITIL®
- Resilience – this is known as *Availability* in ITIL®
- Continuity – known as *ITSCM* in ITIL®
- Security – known as *Security* (wink) in ITIL®

That agreement is technically known as a Service Level Agreement (SLA).

Tip - Continuity is often referred to as DR (Disaster Recovery) in many organizations – the ITIL® term is IT Service Continuity Management (ITSCM).

Of course, these days, with technology being what it is, it is technically feasible to provide very high levels of capacity (storage and throughput) and availability (resilience) – it just costs money! The big question is: are they (the customers) prepared to pay for what they want?

Well that's why we have a negotiation!

Availability Management

Imagine you were dealing with a company that wanted to keep their IT systems going for most of the time. 24 x 7 has become a bit of a buzz-phrase, but it is technically, not really possible. However, it is possible to keep IT systems running even when technical, component failure occurs by utilizing fault-tolerant systems.

There are many technologies that permit us to increase uptime by using the principle of redundancy. This is a simple idea – you have 2 or 3 of certain components in the infrastructure and then when something fails you arrange things to automatically fail-over to the standby unit. Thus you get increased resilience by utilizing the principle of redundancy.

Here are some technologies on the open market that utilize the principle of redundancy:

- Mirroring
- Duplexing
- RAID (Redundant Array of Independent Disks)
- Clustering

All of the above technologies operate on the basis of automatic failover.

Now the Availability Management process seeks to ensure that the appropriate technologies are deployed to achieve the resilience necessary to meet the levels of service defined in the Service level Agreement (SLA) and to do that it produces a plan – the **Availability Plan** is a key output of the Availability Management process.

The process both produces and executes the plan and, of course, the execution is done by raising RFCs (Requests for Change) at the appropriate times in order to get resilient systems deployed in a timely manner.

Capacity Management

The Capacity Management process is responsible for ensuring that the necessary raw processing power - storage facilities, bandwidth etc - are all in place to meet the growing needs of the business. This process is very forward-looking i.e. it is not just concerned with now, but with the future of the business. It actually models the growth of the business to predict how it will grow over time and also attempts to predict the effect of that business growth on the IT infrastructure and the services it supports.

The process actually breaks into three sub-processes (as if we didn't have enough processes to consider already!) but more about them later.

The main output of the process is the **Capacity Plan** which is a plan to introduce the necessary capacity – bigger disks, fatter pipes and faster processors – in a timely manner so that the business is never impacted by the lack of such things. Just like the Availability Management process, this process also produces and executes a plan and, again, the execution is done by raising RFCs.

Tip – Capacity Management is a balancing act: balancing the supply of capacity (storage, bandwidth etc) against demand (the consumption of it) and doing so in a cost-effective manner.

IT Service Continuity Management (ITSCM)

What would happen to the fictitious company we were considering if they were to completely lose all IT facilities; if the building were to burn down, or was flooded or some other major disaster occurred that resulted in the complete loss of all IT facilities? Most companies would eventually go bust without IT. Perhaps some might survive by reverting to manual, paper-based systems, but I think you would agree that these days, with such heavy dependency on IT, most companies would not survive if their key IT systems were not restored within a critical period of time.

If you were to think about this question a little more, you would recognize that some companies would go bust almost immediately. Large financial institutions, for example, would probably not survive for very long without IT. On the other hand, some operations might be able to manage for weeks or possibly even months without IT – sure, there would be a lot of inconvenience, but they would survive.

These questions are right at the heart of the concern of the ITSCM process. It is, naturally, for the business to decide what it wants to happen should such a scenario occur. But it is this process that will come up with the plan (the **ITSCM Plan** – the major output of the process) to achieve what the business wants and to regularly test that plan to ensure that it will run properly should it ever become necessary.

Financial Management

Now, as you know, all of the above (availability, capacity and continuity) costs money! So this process (Financial Management) is responsible for ensuring that the plans produced are properly costed and a budget is secured to implement them. And you know the problems don't you? There never seems to be enough money in the pot. So that's why we have considered these 5 processes together, because they work together – not in isolation – to ensure that the needs of the business are satisfied.

Whenever other processes require financial expertise, it is provided by this process. But the scope of Financial Management relates to three main areas of activity.

Here they are ...

- Budgeting – Securing the necessary funding
- Accounting – Showing where the cash actually went
- Charging – Getting our money back!

Tip – Charging is optional if the organisation is non-profit. But if it is introduced, it can be utilized as a mechanism for shaping user behaviour and can therefore be a very useful tool for managing customer demand.

In addition to the three main activities listed above, this process is involved in many other fiscally-related activities.

Summary of Service Delivery

Processes like Availability, Capacity and ITSCM each have a responsibility to be cost-effective. Let's face it; you can spend a lot of money in these areas. In particular, an incorrectly-sized ITSCM plan could cost the organization substantially. So we can think of the responsibility of these processes as being, to produce an integrated set of plans to meet the needs of the business (or the organisation) in a cost-effective way.

Service Level Management (SLM) is the process responsible for negotiating all of these concerns with the business, or organization, and arriving at an agreement to which all parties subscribe. It is, of course, easier said than done. But it is crucial to the success of IT Service Management because whatever is agreed in the **Service Level Agreement** (SLA) is what the business is actually going to receive.

Higher levels of service invariably mean a higher cost of service provision. The whole thing is up for negotiation before the plans have been finalised, but once the SLA is agreed, the plans – including the financial plan i.e. the **budget** – can be implemented to provide the business the levels of service that are right, given all eventualities.

Let us now move on to discuss 5 more processes – the processes in the old Blue Book (Service Support). These processes are responsible for working together to provide support for what has been documented and agreed in the SLA.

Incident Management

The Incident Management process is carried out by the staff on the Service Desk. The Service Desk staff may or may not, additionally, perform other ITIL® processes, but they will definitely be involved in the Incident Management process.

The goal of this process is to **restore normal service operation as quickly as possible**. Normal service operation being: whatever is defined in the SLA. To help achieve this, the process has access to a key repository – a knowledgebase - which stores details of past incidents and has documented workarounds (temporary measures) that can be invoked at first point of contact to reduce the impact of incidents. A **workaround** is simply a quick-fix or method of avoiding effect of the incident to enable the user to continue working.

The incident may be resolved at first point of contact; however, it may be necessary to involve technical staff working in other functions – often referred to as second-line, third-line support etc. In these cases, the Incident Management process will retain the ownership of the incident, whilst passing the detail to the necessary support staff to deal with the situation. This activity is known as **functional escalation** in ITIL®.

The incident is monitored and tracked by Service Desk staff and eventually it is closed – usually with confirmation from the user that the incident has been resolved.

Problem Management

The Problem Management process is concerned with identifying the underlying causes of incidents. Supposing we have something in the infrastructure that keeps failing repeatedly. There must be some reason that it keeps failing – and that reason is the **problem**.

A number of years ago, there was a situation in which DC10 airplanes were involved in a series of crashes. When investigated, it was found that the design of the cargo hatch door had caused the disasters. In other words, the cargo hatch door design was the problem.

Thinking in terms of cause and effect: **incidents** are an effect; **problems** are a cause. Some organisations call this aspect of Problem Management (the identification of underlying causes) Root-Cause Analysis.

In a nutshell, this process investigates incident data, looking for underlying causes and then it produces either, or both, of two outputs:

- A short-term fix, known as a *Workaround*
- A permanent fix initiated via RFC (Request for Change)

Workarounds are added to the KEDB (Known Error Database) for future reference. This is very useful to Service Desk staff who, as part of the Incident Management process, will search the database for these temporary fixes as incidents are raised. In this way, the impact of incidents that cannot be resolved immediately can often be reduced. This is also a good illustration of how ITIL® processes work together to support each other.

Change Management

Whenever we make a change to the live infrastructure, there is always a corresponding risk to be understood and managed. Change Management is about understanding that risk, assessing it and considering whether or not to proceed with operational change. It is further concerned with the overseeing the successful management of such changes into the live environment.

All changes need to be managed i.e. assessed, authorised, planned, implemented and validated. But the key to getting this discipline operating effectively is to get the right kind of assessments and authorisations in place. That is why there are actually, three types of change recognized by ITIL® and they are each handled slightly differently.

Three Types of Change

- Standard Change – pre-authorised by the process
- Normal Change – goes before the CAB
- Emergency Change – goes before the ECAB

The CAB (Change Advisory Board) is a group of people who meet regularly to discuss proposed changes and to advise on whether or not they should be implemented. Clearly, if your organisation did this every time an RFC was raised, the process would become onerous. That's why we have an ECAB (Emergency CAB) which can be convened very quickly, and it is also why we would almost certainly choose to pre-authorise certain types of change; typically those where the risks are well known and well understood.

Release Management

A release is not a single change, but a collection of changes introduced into the live environment simultaneously and the Release Management (Release and Deployment Management in ITIL® 2011) process works with the Change Management process to ensure the successful introduction (Rollout) of releases into the live environment.

The process considers all aspects of the release including technical and non-technical aspects, including such things as managing user expectations. When dealing with complex changes, a project management approach is definitely preferred, and that's what the Release Management process brings to the party.

An aim of the process is to do fewer, better-managed releases, and this is achieved by packaging releases wherever possible. *Release Packages* consist of *Release Units* and there will typically be more than one Release Unit in a package. Defined in ITIL® as the 'part of the infrastructure normally changed together', a Release Unit is itself a little bundle of changes.

Just to make sure you get the idea of the Release Unit, consider this: imagine you are driving along in your car and your type pops. You have a broken component in the infrastructure (tyre) but you don't actually change the tyre, you change the whole wheel. So you see, the wheel is effectively a Release Unit – the components normally changed together.

Tip - An IT example of a Release Unit is a Microsoft Service Pack – the components (in this case a bundle of software changes) normally changed together.

An important responsibility of Release Management is to ensure that planning and testing, prior to the introduction of a release, is properly completed to ensure the successful transition of releases into the live environment.

Configuration Management

The Configuration Management (Service Asset and Configuration Management in ITIL® 2011) process is concerned with the population and maintenance of the Configuration Management Database (CMDB); a key repository utilized by all IT Service Management processes. It is the place where asset information is stored and also (the thing that differentiates it from an asset database) the relationships between assets. The CMDB thus holds a logical model of the infrastructure.

The introduction of such a database can represent quite a challenge for many organizations, both in terms of effort and cost, but the payoff for creating one is immense. All sorts of useful queries can be answered from the information it holds. For example, we could, very quickly and easily, establish the exact impact of the failure of a particular item (*Configuration Item*) of hardware in terms of the software applications and users that would be affected. Just think how useful that kind of information would be when assessing the impact of a proposed change.

Tip – A Configuration Item, usually abbreviated C.I. is an item held in the CMDB. It can be anything (hardware, software, documents etc) that the organisation wants to manage under change control.

Summary of Service Support

The 5 Service Support processes listed above are instrumental in maintaining the status-quo for the services provided to the organisation. Incident and Problem Management work together to reduce the impact of incidents and to keep things operational.

Change, Release and Configuration Management work together to manage and record changes – large and small – in a controlled manner, ensuring that information in the relevant database is kept up-to-date and can be relied upon by the other service management processes.

The successful resolution of an incident will often involve many or all of the support processes listed: for example, Incident Management will do the initial diagnosis; Problem Management may produce a temporary fix (Workaround); Change Management will get the necessary components swapped; and Configuration Management will record the Change in the CMDB.

Generally speaking, Release Management would not normally be involved in an incident resolution, but it could be: for example, if we have a virus loose on the network and needed to make an **Emergency Change**, then Release Management would be involved because software installation is a part of the scope of that process.

The important thing to understand is that these processes operate in parallel and they feed each other. The outputs of one process may become the inputs of another. For example, when Incident Management or Change Management needs to get something swapped, it raises an RFC (Request for Change) which then goes to the Change Management process.

The above processes make extensive use of the information recorded in databases such as the CMDB and KEDB (Known-Error Database) and they are also responsible for keeping them up-to-date. Configuration Management maintains the CMDB and Problem Management maintains the KEDB.

Tip – The CMDB and KEDB are physical databases that - together with other repositories - make-up the Configuration Management System (CMS) in ITIL® 2011.

The Rewrite

Remember that **all** of the above V2 information <u>also</u> applies to V3 and beyond – it was not made obsolete with the introduction of subsequent versions. The terms *Service Delivery* and *Service Support* are obsolete (i.e. they are V2 terms) but the processes described within those V2 books still exist, though some of them have been slightly renamed.

Here are the Version 2 processes carried forward and slightly renamed to their ITIL®2011 names:

- Incident Management
- Problem Management
- Change Management
- Release & Deployment Management
- Service Asset & Configuration Management
- Service Level Management
- Financial Management for IT Services
- Capacity Management
- Availability Management
- IT Service Continuity Management (ITSCM)

As you can see, apart from a few of the V2 processes - Release Management, Configuration Management and Financial Management – being renamed slightly, they all continue to exist, and function in much the same way, in Version 3 and now in ITIL® 2011.

Release Management becomes Release & Deployment Management. This renaming implies that the process is responsible for deploying new services, as well as performing releases for existing services. Asset Management has always been a sub-set of the Configuration Management discipline and we can see this is now reflected in the new name for the process. Financial Management now becomes Financial Management for IT Services – a nod toward the new service-based accounting guidance to be found in the ITIL® 2011.

We need to go through each of the 26 processes in detail, but before we do that, let's discuss the major difference between Version 2 and subsequent versions of ITIL® – the concept of the Service Lifecycle.

Tip – The Service Lifecycle is now the <u>structure</u> of the new guidance i.e. how the 26 processes are organised.

The Service Lifecycle

The Service Lifecycle is the big change between Version 2 and subsequent versions of ITIL® and – fundamentally – it is a change of structure for the guidance itself.

Services are conceived, designed, transitioned into the live environment and then operated for their useful lives during which time, they are continually improved. That is the reality of life for an IT service. Every service goes through those 5 phases of development and progression and that's how the new version of ITIL® version is structured – that's why the new books bear those titles.

To make sure we understand what the service lifecycle is, let's consider a little analogy: imagine you won a lot of money – so much that you would never need to work again in your entire life. Where would you go? What would you do? Where would you live? Those kinds of questions relate to *strategy*.

Now, staying with our illustration, suppose you decide to live in Australia, would you buy a house or have one built to order? Let's say you decide to have it built, what would you do next? Probably, you would get an architect to draw up the necessary plans – that's *design*. Once your plans are ready, you would get a builder to construct the house for you – that's *transition*. Then you would finally get to live in it – that's *operation*.

Now, if you are married, it is pretty much guaranteed that after you move in, your wife (or you yourself, if you are female) will want to add a conservatory – this is not being sexist; it is just reality. As Billy Conolly once said after he and Pamela had moved into their dream house, "women see something that we men don't – they see potential!" Anyway, adding the conservatory, converting the loft, changing the kitchen etc – that's *CSI* (Continual Service Improvement).

The titles of the books in the guidance are a reflection of the phases of the Service Lifecycle.

The ITIL® 2011 Books

- Service Strategy
- Service Design
- Service Transition
- Service Operation
- Continual Service Improvement (CSI)

So this is how the 26 processes are now organised into the 5 ITIL® publications ...

The following 5 processes are discussed in the Service Strategy book:

- Strategy Management for IT Services
- Financial Management for IT Services
- Service Portfolio Management

- Demand Management
- Business Relationship Management

The following 8 processes are dealt with in the Service Design book:

- Design Coordination
- Capacity Management
- IT Service Continuity Management (ITSCM)
- Availability Management
- Service Catalogue Management
- Information Security management
- Service Level Management
- Supplier Management

The following 7 processes are covered in the Service Transition book:

- Transition Planning
- Release & Deployment Management
- Change Evaluation
- Service Validation & Testing
- Service Asset & Configuration Management
- Change Management
- Knowledge Management

The following 5 processes are defined in the Service Operations book:

- Problem Management

- Incident management
- Request Fulfilment
- Event Management
- Access Management

The following process is in the Continual Service Improvement (CSI) book:

- 7-Step Improvement Process

Now, before we go through each of the 26 processes and 4 functions, let's briefly discuss each of those books at a top level so we can get a feel for what they are about.

Service Strategy

For many people, this book is the most difficult to understand. That's because it is written for those people who are right at the top of the organization who are expected to have some familiarity with general business principles and the understanding of what strategic thinking is about and this is often unfamiliar territory for many IT people.

Now that doesn't mean we can't understand it. Let's face it, if you can understand TCP/IP, then you can cope with just about anything!

So, first off, the book is very cerebral. In order words, it is a lot about thinking. The book itself actually says it will help an organization to be able to 'think and act' in the right way. The essence of the material concerns finding answers to questions like these:

- What services should we offer?
- To whom should we offer them?
- How can we differentiate our service offerings?
- How do we create value for our customers?
- How do we define quality?
- How do we effectively allocate resources?
- How do we resolve conflicting demands?

Strategy – see?

Now then, although the book is concerned with those things, it does not endeavour to provide the answers to those questions. The intention is to provide the guidance that would allow an organization to find the answers to those questions, for itself.

To achieve this, it is suggested that there are four main activities that should be considered as part of an organisation's strategic thinking.

Strategy Management for IT Services Process

- Define the Market
- Develop the Offering
- Develop Strategic Assets
- Prepare for Execution

It is worth bearing in mind that the ITIL® books are written with the intention of being useful to organisations of different sizes and shapes. There are three specific service provides types that the guidance addresses. They are easy to remember; they are called Type 1, Type 2 and Type 2.

Service Provider Types

- Type 1 – Has a single, internal customer
- Type 2 – Has multiple internal customers
- Type 3 – Has external customers

If you think this strategy stuff is not a part of IT, then perhaps you are not alone. Many people think that strategy belongs outside of the scope of IT. But it really depends on the nature of your organization. For a Type 3 provider this strategy stuff definitely is IT because, for such providers, IT *is* the Business.

For a Type 2 provider, IT operates in an internal market. Organisations, naturally, always have a choice when it comes to where to source the IT services it requires. So, here, the recognition of the existence of competitive forces, coupled with a strategic approach to service provision can help to provide us with a competitive edge.

For a Type 3 provider, the strategy guidance enables us to identify market opportunities and correctly position ourselves so that we win new business and retain and even delight existing customers. We do this by providing services that truly do deliver real value to our customers and for which they are more than prepared to pay.

Service Design

OK – now – Service Design: what would you expect this book to be about? Designing services – right?

And so it is. But, it is not *only* concerned with designing services. It is also concerned with the design of other things too. Specifically, it is concerned with the design of the following:

- Design of Services
- Design of Architectures
- Design of Processes
- Design of Measurement Methods
- Design of Tools

Tip: The above list occurs repeatedly throughout the Service Design publication. It is known as the *5 Aspects of Service Design*.

Design of Services

New and existing services come within the scope of this phase of the lifecycle.

The key output of Service Design is a *Service Design Package* (SDP) which contains a complete description of the service to be built and released. This is an important package of documents that contains everything necessary to take the service from design and through the remaining phases of the lifecycle.

The main components of the Service Design Package are shown below:

- Documented Business Requirements
- The Business Case
- The Service Design
- The Specifications
- An Organisational Readiness Assessment
- A Service Lifecycle Plan

Design of Architectures

Underneath our services are the architectures that support it and these include the architectures of Services, Applications and Infrastructures.

The services in our catalogue will conform to an architectural blueprint. For example, some of our services may be reliant upon the existence of other ***enabling services***; and some services may utilise other ***enhancing services*** to add functionality.

In addition to the architecture of services, applications have architectures. For example, an accounting service might consist of the following elements:

- Sales Ledger

- Purchase Ledger
- Nominal Ledger

Finally, infrastructures have architectures consisting of the various hardware elements such as:

- Backbone
- Network Infrastructure
- Hardware Components

Infrastructure includes both a) what is necessary to support the service, and, b) what is needed to manage the service including monitoring and reporting.

Design of Processes

Many people make the mistake (when new to ITIL®) that the books will contain the exact processes they need to implement in their own organisation. In other words, they expect to open the books, find the process steps and then just implement them. This could not be further away from what the guidance recommends.

Although you will find processes described in the books and you will find flowcharts in there too, the ITIL® recommendation is that you should actually design your own processes. That means that the process diagrams are there simply as a reference – they are meant to provide ... *guidance*.

Tip - Many of the better IT Service Management tools – the software you actually use to perform IT Service Management – have the capability for process design built-in.

In designing processes, you need to think about the following *characteristics* that all processes share. They all have the following in common:

- Goal(s)
- KPIs (Key Performance Indicators)
- Roles & Responsibilities
- Process Owner/Manager Role

And in addition, there are *4 Key Characteristics* of all processes:

- They Produce Specific Results
- They are Measurable
- They Deliver Value to Customers/Stakeholders
- They Respond to a Trigger Event

A useful model when designing processes is the RACI model (pronounced racey). It is an example of an authority matrix:

- R ... Responsible
- A ... Accountable
- C ... Consulted
- I ... Informed

The RACI model is a useful tool for mapping the activities of a process onto individual roles. For each of the activities of a process, we need to consider who should be responsible i.e. who gets the job done; who should be accountable i.e. who ensures the job gets done; who should be consulted and who should be informed i.e. which steps require information to be fed into and out of the process.

Note that you might have several, or even many, people responsible for an activity, but only one person would be accountable for each activity. If you think about it, were you to make more than one person as accountable for something, in practice, you would actually have nobody accountable!

Design of Measurements

The idea of continually measuring the results we are producing is a central part of the ITIL® philosophy and, in particular, an integral part of Continual Service Improvement (CSI) which seeks to, constantly, demonstrate objective, measurable improvements.

It is, therefore, important to decide exactly what needs to be measured and how those measurements should be collected and that's what is meant by the design of measurements.

There are very many things you could measure within the following categories:

- Component Measurements
- Process Measurements
- Service Measurements

The above represents different categories of metric that are useful to different audiences.

Component Measurements

The reliability of components in the infrastructure can be measured to produce metrics such as:

- MTBF - Mean Time Between Failures
- MTRS - Mean Time to Restore Service
- MTBSI – Mean Time Between System Incidents

Tip – The MTTR (Mean Time to Repair) metric referred to in V2 is actually a part of the new MTRS metric. But MTRS is a much more useful measurement for many businesses.

Process Measurements

The effectiveness and efficiency of processes can be measured. Effectiveness relates to the goal(s) of the process; efficiency is concerned with doing things in the best possible way. But the main metric for processes is the **Key Performance Indicator** (KPI).

A KPI is something for which you can calculate a numerical value that provides an indication of the effectiveness of the process. If we consider the Incident Management process for example, measurements such as those below can provide a useful indicator of effectiveness:

- % of Calls Correctly Classified
- % of Calls Resolved at First Point of Contact
- % of SLA Breaches

By the way, KPIs can be *qualitative* (a specific category such as red, amber, green) or *quantitative* (a specific number such as a percentage). Remember though that, even for quantitative KPIs, you still need to measure in order to be able to put things into those categories.

ITIL® does not tell you what your KPIs should be; it simply provides suggestions. You decide the KPIs for your own processes yourself.

Service Measurements

If you consider the separate configuration items (hardware, software and anything else) that make up an individual service, you will understand why a failure of any one of them might impact the overall service. This is why it is useful to calculate and report the overall, end-to-end reliability and availability of each service.

One of the central themes of ITIL® is to ensure that we report to each audience in the appropriate way. Service measurements that aggregate measurements from individual configuration items to provide an overall view of the health of a service are particularly useful when reporting to the business.

Design of Tools

There are a couple of obvious choices to be considered when it comes to the design and/or selection of tools:

- Proprietary Solution
- Best of Breed

A proprietary solution provides a 'one-stop-shop' – an integrated approach to the whole of IT Service Management, however, it may or may not be a good fit for your requirements. On the other hand, a best-of-breed approach – mixing and matching different software – may present interesting integration challenges.

The guidance suggests that you should decide upon your own criteria for software selection - including both mandatory and nice-to-have requirements – and then evaluate and rank candidate software, looking for at least an 80% fit to your requirements.

Tip – Tools are also known as Products in ITIL® - they are one of the 4 Ps in Service Design (People, Processes, Products and Partners).

When introducing a new service (or a significant change to an existing service), it is the responsibility of Service Design to include in the Service Design Package (SDP) everything necessary to get the service through transition and into the live environment. So that means there might well be aspects of the design, or redesign, of processes, tools, measurements and architectures included in addition to the actual design of the service.

Service Transition

In ITIL® 2011, the Service Management discipline is a dynamic model, recognizing that managing the complex infrastructures of today necessarily means not just coping with change, but coping with the management of very high levels of change.

Whenever we make a change to the live environment, there is always a corresponding risk involved. Seeking to understand these risks and manage them effectively in the deployment of change is what the Service Transition book is all about.

This phase of the lifecycle receives the Service Design Packages (SDP) from Service Design and it executes a transition project that terminates with the graceful handover, typically after a bedding-in period (known as *Early Life Support*) of a live service to Service Operations.

The transition processes work together to accomplish the successful handover and the important thing is that the transitioned service is virtually guaranteed to work first time and to create a minimum of disturbance and/or disruption to normal business. This guarantee can be made because the processes in this phase of the lifecycle will ensure the new (or changed) service will be first built in a test environment where extensive testing, including testing of the *remediation plan* will be undertaken. The remediation plan (often called a backout plan by many organisations) is a plan for how to recover, in the very unlikely event that things do not go to plan.

Tip – The goal is to introduce the service with 'least disruption for the business' and that means even if it is more work for IT. This is a central principle in ITIL® i.e. that we need to think of the needs of the business (or organisation) first.

Service Operation

There are many references to the creation of value throughout ITIL® - Service Operation is where the value is seen.

There are several competing influences that Service Operations seeks to balance.

- Internal v External Focus
- Proactive v Reactive
- Stability v Responsiveness
- Cost v Quality

Internal v External

An organization that has a view that "the customer is always right" has an external focus; whereas an operation that takes the view that "you can have any colour you want, as long as it's black" has an internal focus.

Proactive v Reactive

The idea of fixing things before they are broken (being proactive) sounds good on the face of it, but we don't want to become the source of unnecessary churn.

Stability v Responsiveness

Similarly, we want to be handle requests for change in an effective and efficient manner, but we don't want to create an unstable environment in the process.

Cost v Quality

Finally, we need to be able to balance the desire to provide a quality service against the cost of providing it – a typical project management concern.

Back to Functions

We have already met the Service Desk function, but there are actually four functions defined in the Service Operations book:

- Service Desk
- Technical Management
- Application Management
- Operations Management

A *function* is the people and tools that are used to execute one or more processes. As we discussed, the Service Desk provides us with a good illustration: the Service Desk function performs the Incident Management process.

These other three functions are responsible for carrying out the other ITIL® processes. Don't get confused about functions: although they are discussed mainly in the Service Operations book, they actually apply to the whole lifecycle. In other words, the people in these functions perform processes in the other lifecycle phases too.

Here are the other three functions:

Technical Management

Technical Management is the function responsible for the *infrastructure*. It provides knowledge, guidance and the actual resources for the maintenance of the infrastructure. The people in this function are our subject matter experts in the area of infrastructure.

Application Management

Application Management is the function responsible for *application software*. It provides knowledge, guidance and the actual resources for the maintenance of applications. It is also the interface to the software development environment. Again, these people are subject matter experts, but in the area of software.

Operations Management

Operations Management is the function responsible for general 'housekeeping' activities such as print jobs, backup etc. It is also responsible for both *Facilities Management* i.e. the management of the physical environment; and *Operations Control* i.e. monitoring. People in this function generally have a wide range of technical skills including both hardware and software.

Continual Service Improvement (CSI)

The idea of continually improving what we are doing in Service Management has always been a part of the ITIL® philosophy. In version 2, it was a specific responsibility of the Service Level Management process. Now, it is the subject of an entire book within the guidance.

The thinking is based on the ideas of William Edwards Deming, who was a leading management thinker around the time of the end of WWII. An American, his ideas were rejected at the time in the USA and embraced by the Japanese. Many analysts have credited the post-war economic revival of Japan as, at least in part, being connected with the adoption of his ideas.

Amongst other things, Deming is famous for the Deming Cycle, or Circle. These days the thinking of Deming, which was truly revolutionary (no pun intended) has been adopted by most progressive organizations in the west. Amongst other things, he believed that the people actually doing the work (whatever that was) were best-placed to make suggestions about process improvement, not the people at the top of the organizational structure.

It now seems quite an obvious truth. But at the time, it *was* a revolutionary idea.

The Deming Cycle

- Plan
- Do
- Check
- Act

The basic idea is that you first plan what you are going to do, and then you do it, whilst collecting performance data at the same time. You analyse your results (check) and finally, you make some changes (improvements) based on that analysis. Once you have made an improvement, you take actions to consolidate your position before thinking about going round the cycle again.

There are many things to which you can apply this improvement philosophy including processes, services, systems, tools, technology and so on. Thus, Continual Service Improvement (CSI) is said to operate across the lifecycle contributing to the delivery of ever-increasing levels of value to the business.

It might not be entirely evident at first, but the Deming Cycle is deeply embedded into much of the ITIL® philosophy and the more you look for it, the more you can find it. Most ITIL® processes involve planning, doing and checking. The notion of initiating improvements based on measurements, then, effectively completes the cycle and that is the subject of this book in the guidance.

Essentially, the overall approach to CSI involves answering these questions:

- What's the Vision? – Set by Strategy
- Where are we now? – A Baseline Assessment
- Where do we want to be? – A Target
- How do we get there? – A Plan
- Have we arrived? – A Measurement
- How to maintain Momentum? – Next Improvement

The above model is not an ITIL® process; it is actually described as an approach – *The CSI Approach*.

You can use that same basic approach for improving Services, Processes and whole Lifecycle Phases. Even, to go a step further, for the improvement of the Service Management discipline as a whole.

The ITIL Processes

At this point, we should have a pretty good overview of IT Service Management discipline based on the ITIL® guidance. We have encountered processes and functions and we have discussed enough processes to have developed a reasonable grasp of what is being done.

The official stance is that no process is more important than any other and there is certainly an argument for that view. However, my own opinion is that if you can first grasp the foregoing, you have the essence - the heart – of what ITIL® is all about.

However, the next step is to look at all 26 processes in turn, put some more flesh on the bones, so to speak, and add in all of the bells and whistles. So this section looks at each of the ITIL® processes in turn following the structure of the lifecycle.

So, here we go ...

Strategy Management for IT Services

Here are the steps of the process:

- Define the Market
- Develop the Offerings
- Develop Strategic Assets
- Prepare for Execution

Define the Market

This is concerned with understanding who the customer actually is. This may seem ridiculous, but a thorough understanding of the customer and the market in which the customer exists is an absolutely essential part of crafting a service strategy.

Naturally, there are different types of organization and different types of customer. You remember that ITIL® defines three different types of service provider, operating within different markets.

- Type 1 ... Single Internal Customer
- Type 2 ... Multiple Internal Customers
- Type 3 ... External Customers

A *Type 1* service provider is an organization that services a single internal customer – in other words, the Business, or the Organisation itself, is the customer. For many such operations, the concept of the Business (or Organisation) being a customer is an alien thought however, the notion of the customer is pivotal to the whole idea of being a service provider. Service providers have customers – whether or not they actually pay any money for the services they receive. That idea is central to Service Management.

Type 2 service providers also service an internal market, but they operate as an autonomous entity providing services to various Business Units. Generally, Type 2 providers do recognize they are operating within some kind of market. However, competition does not really exist in the true sense of the external market. Though, perhaps some would argue that the constant threat that the organisation may choose to outsource the provision of some services does act to provide some kind of commercial driver.

Type 3 service providers offer their services to customers on the open market. They charge for the services they offer and are in the business of service provision in order to make a profit.

Charging may also be implemented by Types 1 and 2 providers even though, in those cases, the customer is internal. The decision of whether or not to do this is a policy decision. But, should the organization's policy permit the charging of internal customers, the mechanism can prove useful as a means of shaping user behaviour.

Develop the Offerings

This activity is concerned with understanding what the customer wants and needs. Customers don't buy products or services – they buy solutions. So exactly what solutions will we, as a service provider, be offering? That question is the essence of this activity.

The guidance suggests that an organization should be concerned with aligning its portfolio of services with *Market Spaces* – these are simply opportunities that exist to develop service offerings for the target market. Naturally, in order to do that, we first need to spend some time actually identifying those opportunities (Market Spaces).

The guidance suggests starting off by coming up with an 'Outcome-Based' definition of the services to be offered. In other words, what exactly would be the specific benefits of each of the services that could be offered? Once we have a whole set of these 'Outcome-Based' definitions, the opportunity (Market Space) will become apparent.

The Service Portfolio – a new concept brought in at Version 3 – is a key information system that is essential to this process. As we shall see, the portfolio is quite central to the whole idea of the service lifecycle.

The identification of market spaces is an activity that is crucial to subsequent decisions related to where and how to commit resources. Resources are a limited commodity, so good decisions on where to invest them is a vitally important aspect of strategy. Information in the portfolio therefore begins with the identification of Market Spaces.

Develop Strategic Assets

Strategic Assets provide the raw material for creating a service. As service providers we combine them to create services that deliver value to customers. There are two types of service assets – *resources* and *capabilities*.

Resources are as tangible assets. They are things the organisation can <u>use</u> to achieve its goals, such as hardware, people, money etc. Capabilities are intangible assets. They are the various things the organization can actually <u>do</u> such as management, organization, skills, knowledge etc. Collectively, resources and capabilities are referred to as *service assets*.

As we are continually challenged to deliver higher levels of service, we respond by developing the ability to meet those challenges and this necessarily involves the development or acquisition of further resources and capabilities.

The strategy guidance also discusses the discipline of IT Service Management itself and the case for viewing it as a

strategic asset of the organization. If we can get better at the business of IT Service Management, it argues, then IT Service Management itself will become a strategic asset of the organization.

Tip – Be aware that the guidance refers to IT Service Management as a whole in several places. Above is an example of this i.e. the idea of IT Service Management becoming a Strategic Asset.

Prepare for Execution

In Preparing for Execution, we are concerned with the crafting of strategic intent; there are two parts to it – Strategic Assessment and Strategy Generation.

Strategic Assessment - concerns thorough self-reflection. In other words, what is it that we, as a service provider, already do well? Understanding what we already do well is likely to reveal a core of differentiation – the understanding of what makes our services do well.

Strategy Generation - in order to generate a strategy, *Mintzberg's 4 Ps* provide a useful reference point. His 4 Ps are: **perspective**, **position**, **plan** and **patterns**.

- Perspective – the operation needs a vision
- Position – that basis on which we will compete
- Plan – including Critical Success Factors (CSF)
- Patterns – develop consistency in actions taken

Tip - Be aware that there are another set of 4 Ps in the Service Design book (People, Processes, Products & Partners). Make sure you don't get them confused.

Finally, out of all of this reflection – strategy involves thinking as well as acting - comes the strategy itself i.e. the basic stance of the organization for the services it will offer. Will we be the cheapest in the market; will we become the quality offering; will be become the most trusted source for our services? These questions relate to *positioning* and, along with our *perspective* (vision) they affect our *plan*.

Financial Management for IT Services

The best way to think of what the process does is that it provides the necessary financial advice, guidance and rigor where it is needed by other parts of Service Management. For example, supposing that the Problem Management process needs to make a Business Case to justify some additional spending. The Problem Manager, who might not be well-versed in financial matters, may need some assistance with that – well this process would be provider of that help.

There are three main activities in Financial Management:

- Budgeting
- Accounting
- Charging

Budgeting

Budgeting is the business of predicting the costs that will be incurred for the fiscal year ahead or, in other words, it is financial planning. It is the business of putting a price on the integrated set of plans (Capacity, Availability etc produced by Service Design) that will be necessary to support the business for the year ahead.

Accounting

Accounting is showing where the money has been spent – this is described as providing **operational visibility**. Accounting should be introduced after Budgeting and before Charging. It is easy to understand why: once we know how much a particular department is costing, it is a useful prerequisite to preparing and issuing the bill.

Charging

Charging is an optional area in ITIL®. There are pros and cons to be considered for Type 1 and Type 2 providers. However, if the organization does decide to charge the Business for the provision of IT Services, the guidance on how to do it effectively is provided.

Charging Policies

- Zero Balance – Cost Recovery
- Cost Plus – Making a Profit
- Cost Minus – Making a Loss (Subsidised Service)
- Going Rate – Internal Comparison
- Market Rate – External Comparison
- Fixed Rate – Arbitrary

The optional activity – charging – depends on what kind of organization you actually have and whether or not it is appropriate. However, even in some operations where the business (customer) is internal, charging for the provision of IT services can be of great benefit. At least it serves as a constant reminder to non-IT staff that technology costs the operation money.

As discussed, there are definite pros and cons to introducing charging. ITIL® essentially stays out of the argument. Basically, you decide what is right for your organization and ITIL® gives you the tools to implement charging if it is appropriate for your operation.

Here are the charging policies you might consider …

- No Changing – it's still a policy decision
- Cost Minus – making a loss
- Zero Balance – recovering costs
- Cost Plus – making a profit
- Market Rate – an external price comparison
- Going Rate – an internal price comparison
- Fixed Rate – an arbitrary charge

Most of these policies make sense from their names. Making a loss sounds a bit silly, but that is the essence of what is entailed in providing a subsidized service. The **Going Rate** is a term to describe an internal comparison i.e. what others are charging internally. It might also be based on opportunity-cost i.e. what you could charge someone else for the resources you have committed.

Service Portfolio Management

The Service Portfolio is a central concept in ITIL® 2011. It represents the commitment of the organization to market spaces (opportunities).

The steps of the process are as follows:

- Define
- Analyse
- Approve
- Charter

This is where a Service begins its life as an idea. It is where the idea is evaluated to determine whether or not it is a good idea i.e. the **Business Case** is prepared, and it is where the idea is eventually approved or rejected. The process takes the concept from a service definition to the actual chartering (allocation) of resources.

In analyzing the proposition for a new service, the process would consider the following questions.

Does the proposed new service help us to:

- Run the Business
- Grow the Business
- Transform the Business

The preparation of a Business Case provides the necessary justification – often financial – for taking the idea forward. A **Net Present Value** (NPV) calculation is often useful for determining the expected **Return on Investment** (ROI) in the preparation of a Business Case. Remember that Financial Management for IT Services process can provide assistance with this type of calculation.

Once the service reaches the chartered status (i.e. resources are committed) the service leaves the **Service Pipeline** and enters the **Service Catalogue**. The catalogue is the customer-visible portion of the Service Portfolio. At this stage, the service is still to be designed and built; however, the decision has now been taken to commit to the delivery of the service.

The process itself is cyclic in nature - continually seeking to validate the accuracy of the information contained within the Service Portfolio and periodically refresh the business cases.

Demand Management

Demand Management is closely related to Capacity Management. However, Demand Management is more forward-looking seeking to operate on the causes of demand i.e. the customer. Capacity Management is specifically responsible for ensuring we have sufficient capacity (bandwidth, storage, throughput etc) in the infrastructure.

The Demand Management process is concerned with understanding and influencing the customer demand for the services that the business offers. Now, of course, there are subtle differences when it comes to the different supplier types.

For Type 1 and 2 suppliers, this means understanding the demand for whatever it is that the business produces. For example a toy manufacturer produces toys and Demand Management would be attempting to understand the factors operating within the external market that create demand for those products - that's why this process is in the Service Strategy book.

Every Christmas, for example, the demand for toys increases – that is known as a *Pattern of Business Activity* (PBA). This process seeks to understand those PBAs and regulate or influence them. If demand for our products drops, then the introduction of special offers, for example, can help to stimulate consumption; if demand is greater than the ability of the business to respond, then an increase in price can help to both curtail demand and optimise profit.

For Type 3 suppliers – where IT *is* the business – the customer demand for the products the business produces is the same thing as the demand for IT services since IT services, in that situation, are the product. However, the same considerations apply and it remains vitally important to properly match supply against demand.

The outputs of this process include **policies** that define working practices including constraints that are designed to influence or regulate consumption of the product:

- Financial Constraints – e.g. Differential Charging
- Physical Constraints – e.g. Flexible Working Hours

Financial constraints might include, for example, **differential charging** - charging more for our services at peak times and less at off-peak times – as a means of shaping user behaviour. Physical constraints might include, for example, the adoption of flexible working hours as a means of displacing demand over time. Such policies would then be carried out by other processes e.g. Financial Management.

In addition, this process is concerned with stimulating demand for the consumption of our services.

Services are composed of various elements and by adding on additional functionality (also called *Utility*) and/or **Warranty** – a service guarantee - the service provider can create differentiated offerings. This is important because, if we are to get people to buy our services, rather than those offered by the competition, we need to give them a very good reason to do so.

For example, an email service might consist of the following elements:

- Email Service
- Superior Spam Filtering
- 15 Gb of Free Storage

The combination of these elements becomes our differentiated email service offering.

By the way, if you have a gmail account, you will recognise that although Google don't actually sell their email service, they actually did include the above elements in the package and that is probably why you have the account.

Business Relationship Management

As service providers, we want to be successful and that, of course, means we want people to buy our services. To achieve that objective, we really need to understand why people buy them and/or why they don't buy them. We may think we understand, but that is not quite the same thing.

In order to be successful as a service provider, we need to truly understand our customers. When we can get our minds deep into the businesses of our key customers and understand them so well that we could probably go and work there, then we develop a unique perspective on our customer's needs that is priceless.

This perspective enables us to develop services that truly do serve the needs of our customers in a way that not only differentiates us from the competition, but that really creates value for our customers. When we can do that, there really is every reason that those customers should buy from us. The role of Business Relationship Manager is tasked with developing that perspective for our key accounts – some organisations call this role the Account Manager. But don't get confused: although we do want to sell services, this role is much more than a sales role.

The Business Relationship Manager represents our organisation to our customers and also does the reverse i.e. it represents our customer's interests internally. This role would work closely with the owner of the Service Catalogue (Product Manager) to get ideas for new services properly considered via the Service Portfolio Management process.

Tip – The Product Manager is the owner of the Service Catalogue or a sub-set of the catalogue known as a *Line of Service*. Large organisations would have more than one Product Manager. Don't get this role confused with the owner of the Service Catalogue Management process.

Design Coordination

In much the same way that there is an overarching spine process (Transition Planning & Support) that glues together the other process activities within Service Transition, so we have an equivalent process here in Service Design. This process functions much like the Project Office in PRINCE2 (Project Management guidance).

For each new service design, the process performs the following activities:

- Planning & Coordination
- Review & Handover

Planning and coordination involves coordinating the design activities carried out by all the other design processes. When all design activities are complete, this process (Design Coordination) is responsible for conducting a final review of the design, specifications and plans. It then assembles the SDP (Service Design Package) and formally hands it over to Service Transition.

In addition to the above, the process is also concerned with setting design policy, managing design risks, planning the best use of resources and capabilities across multiple projects and improving the effectiveness and efficiency of Service Design as a whole.

Capacity Management

Often described as a 'balancing act', Capacity Management is responsible for ensuring that sufficient capacity - bandwidth, storage and throughput – is available to support the current and future needs of the organization.

The process seeks to balance supply against demand – working with the Demand Management process – and also seeks to balance cost against capacity. In other words, the process recognizes that you can always purchase more capacity (storage, bandwidth etc) but it might not always be wise to do so.

For example, it doesn't matter how big the user's mailboxes are, they will always fill them up. That's a fact; and it is an application of Parkinson's Law to the IT world. So providing bigger mailboxes is definitely not the answer to that particular capacity issue. Instead, we need to be more concerned with affecting user-behaviour – that's what is meant by Demand Management.

The process beaks-down into three sub-processes:

- Business Capacity Management
- Service Capacity Management
- Component Capacity Management

Business Capacity Management

This sub-process is concerned with the future of the business. It is responsible for modelling business growth and ensuring that provision for that growth is properly planned. It has access to important business data including the Business Plan and it is required to ensure that sufficient capacity always exists to cope with the various alternative futures the business may be contemplating at any particular time.

Service Capacity Management

This sub-process is closely related to the subject of Demand Management. Demand Management is all about trying to understand varying customer demand for services and ensuring that adequate capacity (storage/throughput) exists to handle it. Sometimes this is achieved by simply shaping (regulating) user behaviour. A simple example of this would be the introduction of flexible working hours to naturally spread demand over a longer period. Service Capacity Management is concerned with the end-to-end provision of capacity for the services offered to the business.

Component Capacity Management

This sub-process is concerned with the bits and bytes of the infrastructure. It is concerned with monitoring file-systems as they grow; it is concerned with monitoring bandwidth; it is concerned with monitoring processors

(CPUs). It looks for capacity bottlenecks and ensures that solutions are introduced.

All three sub-processes are involved in the following activities to a great or lesser extent:

- Tuning
- Modelling
- Application-Sizing

Tuning

Tuning involves monitoring the infrastructure, analyzing the gathered data, tuning variables in the infrastructure and implementing various control policies.

There are very many variables in the infrastructure that could be tuned to optimize the provision of capacity. For example, log file sizes might be reduced; TCP/IP Windows might be adjusted and so on.

Modelling

There are several different types of modelling activities the process would be involved in including *analytical modelling* (based on mathematical principles like queuing theory). Here, the optimum required capacity to cope with the current demand for services could be identified and perhaps even brought on-stream seamlessly and automatically for example, by utilising technologies such as VMware.

Application Sizing

This activity attempts to predict the effect of the introduction of a new application into the existing infrastructure.

Capacity Management Information System (CMIS)

The process makes use of the CMIS to record information from the three sub-processes and to model the growth of the business over time.

Tip – Don't get confused between the CMIS and the CMS; they are separate information systems that both live inside the SKMS (Service Knowledge Management System).

The Capacity Plan

The *capacity plan* is a key output of the process which considers the possible alternative futures for the business and makes capacity recommendations for each.

Generally, this is an annual activity tied up with the production of the annual budget by Financial Management; however, the capacity plan may be revised should it be required to plan for the support of new services to be introduced into the live environment.

Information Security Management

It is the people at the top of the organization - normally, the directors - that are ultimately responsible for the organisation's data. This process is concerned with fulfilling certain of the important legal obligations of the organisation in relation to the collection, storage and distribution of its data.

The Information Security Management process is concerned with the confidentiality, integrity, availability and authenticity of data.

- Confidentiality – only the required people can see it
- Integrity – the trustworthy-ness of the data
- Availability – there when it's needed
- Authenticity – external data transactions can be trusted

As such, the process has close links with Availability Management (concerned with availability issues) and Access Management (concerned with confidentiality issues).

It is specifically responsible for devising the **Information Security Policy** (ISP) which should be an integral part of the overall Security Policy of the organization. Communication of the policy is an important responsibility of the process. Let's face it, one of the most common reasons that people fail to follow organisational policy is that they don't know what it is.

The process is also concerned with identifying and assessing risks relating to data security and imposing security controls to mitigate against such risks. The process uses the **CRAMM** (CCTA Risk Analysis and Management Method) technique to evaluate and manage risks.

The process uses the Security Management Information System (SMIS) to keep a record of policies, reports, controls and risks.

Tip – The Information Security Management process is one of several ITIL® processes involved in Risk Management; it is worth noting that both ITSCM and Availability Management are also involved.

Availability Management

Availability Management is concerned with resilience – ensuring that we have sufficient resilience (fault-tolerance) in the infrastructure to cope with component failure in such a manner (by masking the effect) that the SLA (Service Level Agreement) remains unaffected.

Availability is defined as the percentage of Agreed Service Time that a Service is actually available. The calculation is pretty straightforward:

$$\frac{\text{Actual Time}}{\text{Agreed Service Time}} \quad X \quad 100$$

So notice that 100% availability is not the same thing as 24 x 7. In fact 24 x 7 might be a nice buzz-phrase, but technically, it is not really achievable in practice. The best many operations hope to achieve is 99.999% availability – often referred to as the five nines of availability.

You could spend a lot of money making use of the principle of redundancy to increase resilience by eradicating *single points of failure* (SPOF), for example by using technologies such as RAID, clustering, mirroring, duplexing etc. So be aware that the process is not trying to increase resilience to the <u>maximum</u> levels possible, but it is very specifically concerned with providing the level of resilience that is needed to meet the requirements specified in the SLA – and to do so in a cost-effective manner.

Techniques

Here are some techniques used by Availability Management:

- CFIA – Component Failure Impact Analysis
- FTA – Fault Tree Analysis
- SFA – Service Failure Analysis
- TOP - Technical Observation Post

CFIA is a method of assessing the impact of component failures i.e. answering the question: which services would be affected if a specific component in the infrastructure were to fail? The analysis provides the answer to this question for each component in the infrastructure. The usefulness of the technique is that it can help to identify critical components that may need additional resilience to be added.

FTA is an analysis technique that uses logic gates to represent the infrastructure. It allows the application of logic to be applied to quickly assess the knock-on consequences of the failure of a component of the infrastructure.

SFA involves getting a team of technical experts together following a service outage in order to take on-board any lessons that have been learned during the failure and the process of restoring normal service operation.

TOP also involves getting a group of technical experts together to make recommendations, but this is done during the event rather than afterward.

Metrics

There are a number of standard metrics used by the process:

- MTBF – Mean Time Between Failures
- MTRS – Mean Time to Restore Service
- MTBSI – Mean Time Between Service Incidents

The Availability Plan

The Availability Plan is the main output of the process. It will be updated regularly - at least annually, in line with budgets, but perhaps more regularly as appropriate for the organisation. Any proposed new services or changes to existing services may impact the Availability Plan, so representation of this process on the CAB is desirable.

The actual changes required to implement the plan will also be subject to change control in the normal way i.e. Requests for Change (RFC) will be raised by Availability Management process, and go to the Change Management process for consideration in the normal way.

Service Catalogue Management

This process is simple and straight-forward - it concerns the production and maintenance of the service catalogue; the service catalogue being the customer-visible portion of the service portfolio. It may offer several different views of the same information, typically a business view (Business Service Catalogue) and a technical view (Technical Service Catalogue). Ensuring that an accurate service catalogue is produced and maintained has many benefits to other areas of ITIL®.

The service catalogue contains complete details of all the services in the live environment and those being prepared to run i.e. in the design phase. New services enter the catalogue when resources have been committed to the project i.e. when the service has reached the *chartered* state - see the Service Portfolio Management Process (above).

Services consist of a **Core Service** (CSP) plus **Service Level Packages** (SLP) that provide additional levels of utility (functionality) and/or warranty (gold, silver, bronze etc). These additional levels of warranty/utility are purchase options; and the idea is to manage the service 'as a product' hence the ITIL® role of Product Manager. The availability of different service level packages for the same core service technically makes the offering a **Line of Service** (LOS).

Product Managers are the experts on *Lines on Service* and are responsible for the following:

- Developing and managing services through the lifecycle

- Managing services as a product over their entire lifecycle

- Subject matter experts on Lines of Service (LOS) and the Service Catalogue

- Coordination and focus around the Service Catalogue, of which they maintain ownership

Product Managers work closely with Business Relationship Managers (BRM) who represent the customer - in what many organisations call an Account Manager capacity; and we can think of the Service Catalogue as providing substance for discussions with prospects around the product offerings in the catalogue. Business Relationship Managers are responsible for mapping user profiles onto Service Level Packages in the catalogue i.e. making appropriate product recommendations.

IT Service Continuity Management (ITSCM)

The ITSCM process needs to be seen as part of an organisation's wider Business Continuity Management (BCM) process. In other words, ITSCM is the IT part within BCM. It is concerned with ensuring that the key IT systems either remain operational, or are restored to normal operation within agreed business timescales, in the event of a major disaster such as fire, flood, terrorism etc.

In order to achieve the goal of immunity or restoration, the mission-critical services and systems need to be first identified - in ITIL®, these key services are known as **Vital Business Functions** (VBF) - and the overall approach needs to be agreed with the business. In order to do this, a **Business Impact Analysis** (BIA) would be carried out seeking to address the question of what would happen to the business in the event of a catastrophic loss of IT services. This analysis provides important input into the decision concerning the recovery strategy that needs to be employed.

There are a number of strategies in common use. Each of these strategies concerns recovering IT services with a specific timescale.

Getting the **ITSCM Plan** 'right-sized' for the operation is a vitally important aspect of the exercise. These days, with technology so advanced, it is possible to provide the business with a whole host of options for recovery. These include ...

- Immediate Recovery (Hot Standby) – instant or almost instant recovery

- Fast Recovery (also Hot Standby) – recovery in less than 24 hours

- Intermediate Recovery (Warm Standby) – recovery within 24 – 72 hours

- Gradual Recovery (Cold Standby) – recovery in greater than 72 hours

The options above are popular and pragmatic and most organisations have a plan that would fit into one of the options because they are doable. There are other (less popular) options though, including :

- Do Nothing – a plan for the business to go bust!

- Reciprocal Arrangements – with another company/operation i.e. you can use our IT if we can use yours.

- Manual Backup – revert to paper systems (yuk!)

There are many options to choose between for providing technology and architectures that are capable of being recovered very quickly - in fact, possibly even instantly - so such considerations should ideally be built-in to the design of the infrastructure from the outset. However, the cost of provision of a highly resilient infrastructure is a second factor to be taken into consideration in the construction of an appropriate strategy for ITSCM because, of course, our budget is not unlimited,

The business needs to recognise that there is a trade-off between investment costs and achievable recovery times. Understanding this trade-off and communicating it together with a proper assessment of business impacts allows the business to choose a recovery strategy that is right-sized for the organisation.

This process is responsible for recommending that strategy and then planning accordingly. The ITSCM plan is a key output of the process, and regular review and testing of the plan are key activities. Testing can take different forms, from simple walk-through reviews to full-blown testing with everyone in the operation involved in simulating a disaster and invoking recovery procedures.

Good times to test the plan include: immediately after the initial formulation; regularly (at least annually); and following any major change.

Service Level Management

The Service Level Management process is responsible for negotiating and agreeing **Service Level Agreements** (SLA) and **Operational Level Agreements** (OLA). The responsibility for negotiating Contracts/Underpinning Contracts, which was part of this process in V2, has now been stripped away; and is now the responsibility of the Supplier Management process.

A Service Level Agreement is a written agreement between the Customer and Service Provider that documents service level targets. An Operational Level Agreement is an agreement between internal technical teams, and it underpins the SLA. A Contract or **Underpinning Contract** (UC) is a legally-binding agreement with an external organisation that also underpins the SLA.

The process begins with documenting **Service Level Requirements** (SLR) - these represent the warranty (guarantee) aspects of the service. After the necessary negotiations, the process will arrive at an understanding with the business, or organisation, that will form a draft agreement and will become the basis of the SLA itself.

Three Types of SLA

   - *Customer Based* - focused around the needs of one particular customer

- *Service Based* - focused on an individual service

  - *Multi-Level* - a more complex structure with different levels for different services and/or customer groups

The Service Level Management process works in conjunction with other processes to arrive at an appropriate agreement. In addition to the Supplier Management process, which is responsible for negotiating the necessary contracts with external operations that underpin the SLA, the Availability Management process is responsible for the necessary planning to achieve the agreed levels of service, and the Financial Management process is responsible for budgeting for any necessary investment identified by the Availability Management process.

Once an SLA is in place, this process (SLM) is concerned with monitoring and measuring service level achievements, and broadcasting them to all relevant parties. Additionally, SLAs are regularly reviewed with the customer and updated where and whenever necessary.

Supplier Management

Supplier Management is responsible for sourcing, vetting, negotiating contracts and monitoring the performance of external partners in Service Management, and renewing or terminating contracts as necessary. A contract is a legally-binding agreement and we will have them in place with external organisations we are working with. Some contracts are said to underpin the Service Level Agreement (SLA) and such a contract is therefore known as an Underpinning Contract (UC).

Previously, in V2, the activities of this process (Supplier Management) were a responsibility of the Service Level Management process, but from V3 on, Supplier Management is a process in its own right. A good decision, because the skills necessary for contract negotiations with external organisations are quite different to those required for the internal negotiations with which SLM is most concerned.

The process maintains all the necessary contract detail in the Supplier and Contacts Management Information System (SCMIS) - a component of the SKMS.

Transition Planning

When performing a service transition such as the introduction of a new service into the live environment, we are really involved in running a transition project and we therefore need a process to be responsible for the top-level planning of the project. In a nut-shell, that is what this process does. It ensures there is a coordinated approach to service transitions and it effectively operates in much the same way as the Project Office within the PRINCE2 guidance.

Tip – PRINCE2 (Projects in Controlled Environments) is a source of Best Practice for Project Management and contains relevant additional guidance for Service Transition.

As a top-level process, it is accountable for the overall transition goals including delivering the service within agreed costs and timescales – a typical project management message that you may recognise i.e. to ensure the project comes in on time and within budget and also ensures the service does what it should do (quality).

Specific responsibilities of the process include:

- Planning and Coordination of All Transitions
- Establishing Services within agreed Parameters (Time, Quality and Cost)

- Identifying and Managing Risks

In particular, *coordination* involves making best use of resources and capabilities, balancing them across the various transition projects that may be in progress at any particular time, and also working with project managers responsible for business change to integrate service transitions within the overall business change process.

Release & Deployment Management

The main thing to remember about this process is that, in addition to actually introducing releases, it is also responsible for ensuring that the necessary testing that precedes a release is properly completed. Now don't get confused, there is a separate Service Testing and Validation process that typically performs the testing, but Release & Deployment Management <u>ensures</u> it gets done.

The reason for this distinction is obvious when you consider the stated purpose of the process i.e. to deploy releases whilst 'protecting the integrity of the existing services'. This basically means that we do not engage in deployments unless we have a very high degree of confidence that the transition will be successful first time. And when you think about that, it is obvious why testing is necessary and therefore why this process is accountable. Quite simply, it is the only way we can possibly have that level of confidence.

Three Types of Release:

- *Major Release* - new hardware and/or software with significantly increased functionality
- *Minor Release* - minor updates
- *Emergency Release* - quick fix for bugs and/or known errors

Release Policy

It is important that the organisation's release policy spells out the correct balance between cost, stability and agility. For some services, stability may need to be maximised even if that means more testing and therefore more costs are incurred. For other services, it may be more important to deliver functionality very quickly (i.e. being agile) even if that means stability might be jeopardised – it is all a matter of policy.

Release Options

- Push or Pull
- Big Bang or Phased
- Automated or Manual

When considering release options, the process will consider a 'push' versus a 'pull' approach i.e. whether to 'push' out the release to users or to install on demand. It will consider a 'big-bang' versus a 'phased' approach i.e. whether to do it all in one go or to use several separate release phases. Finally, it will consider whether to use an 'automated' or a 'manual' method of handling the release.

Change Evaluation

If you think about the progress of a change or release from the initial request through to the actual deployment, it is clear that there are various distinct stages that may each be required to be evaluated and approved; for example, build, test and deployment.

Even within the deployment stage alone, where the deployment option chosen is a phased approach, there may be a need to approve the progress of the deployment from phase 1 to phase 2 and so on. Supposing that, despite our extensive testing, the phase 1 deployment has not gone quite so well as we expected, should we go on to phase 2 or should we roll back? There could, of course, be a case for either decision. But the point is that an evaluation would be necessary in order to make the right decision – and that's what this process does.

Each phase of a release typically involves a little cycle consisting of *baseline*, *deploy* and *evaluate* activities. Release and Deployment Management does the deployment and this process (Change Evaluation) does the evaluation i.e. it provides a Change Report so the Change Management process is equipped to authorise or reject the progress of the release.

Note: For completeness, in a phased release, it is the Service Asset and Configuration Management process (discussed later) that performs the *baselining* activity.

Service Validation & Testing

There are all kinds of tests that might be carried out in support of a service transition including (but not limited to):

- Functional Testing ... Does it work properly?
- Operation Testing ... Will it work in the live environment?
- Performance Testing ... Is it fast enough?
- Integration Testing ... Does it work with other systems/services?

Quite simply, this is the process that performs the testing. It is a lifecycle wide process and can therefore be used at any time to validate the 'fitness for purpose' (utility) and/or 'fitness for use' (warranty) of any service. However, the process is used extensively by the Release and Deployment Management process in the support of a release.

We said that testing was very important when performing any kind of significant change and that Release and Deployment Management was accountable for the testing – and this is true - but this process (Service Validation & Testing) actually maintains the test environment (including test data, test scripts and test models) and actually performs the necessary testing, providing reports that are utilised by the Release and Deployment Management process.

Service Asset & Configuration Management

This process is responsible for the initial population and subsequent maintenance of the CMDB(S) – you CAN have more than one (for example, a testing CMDB and a live CMDB) if it is appropriate to your organisation. Either way, the CMDB(S) live inside the SKMS (Service Knowledge Management System).

Here are the process steps:

- Planning
- Identification
- Control
- Status Reporting
- Verification

The introduction of this process and the corresponding database does need to be thought through very carefully before actually starting, and typically, the Planning stage of the process might take approximately 3-6 months – perhaps a little less these days, now that we have such excellent tools available for auto-discovery and recording of complex infrastructures.

Identification is the business of deciding exactly which items in the infrastructure will come under **Configuration**

Control i.e. which items will become Configuration Items (CIs) - and then labelling them.

Control involves the population and maintenance of the CMDB itself. The step is called 'control' because it is synonymous with Change Control i.e. nothing will get changed in the live environment without a record of the change being made – hence changes are controlled.

Status Reporting (also known as Status Accounting) permits a complete and accurate record – a cradle to grave history – to be generated for any item (CI) under configuration control, so we can see exactly where any CI is within its lifecycle, and we can also see any planned updates.

Finally, *Verification* involves the regular auditing of the live environment to ensure that it matches the logical model held within the database.

Change Management

Change is initiated by the raising of an RFC (request for Change) and, in principle, anyone in the organization can raise one – this includes users. The process evaluates RFCs, considering whether or not to approve them for implementation.

As we previously discussed, all changes need to be managed i.e. assessed, authorised, planned, implemented and validated. But, in order to strike the correct balance between maintaining control of change whilst remaining flexible and agile so that we don't unnecessarily obstruct change, there are actually, three types of change recognized by ITIL® and they are each handled slightly differently.

Three Types of Change

- Standard Change – pre-authorised by the process
- Normal Change – goes before the CAB
- Emergency Change – goes before the ECAB

Standard Change does not need approval – it is simply performed and recorded in the CMDB. This allows for changes to be pre-approved where the risks are well understood; for example, a request for a new printer or a replacement monitor. Such changes would typically not need to be discussed at the CAB. Having said that, the decision about how to define the changes that actually follow which of the three routes mentioned above is a policy decision and it may vary from organisation to organisation.

Normal changes are discussed by the *Change Advisory Board* (CAB) which will make the recommendation. Strictly, the approval of change is done by the *Change Authority* (in practice, this is often the Change Manager). The *Change Manager* role is an important role and, in many organizations, the role will have overall accountability for all aspects of change. In addition, part of the responsibility of the Change Manager role is to 'chair' the CAB.

Tip – In ITIL® all processes have *owners*. The Change Manager is the owner of the Change Management process and this role has overall accountability for the process.

The *ECAB* (Emergency CAB) is effectively a subset of the CAB and it meets to discuss *emergency changes*. Again the Change Manager will effectively 'chair' the meeting however, this meeting might be quite informal – in practice, it is often a telephone conference conversation.

Knowledge Management

Knowledge Management is 'getting the right information to the right people at the right time' so they can make the right decision. That statement is very easy to remember and it is also a very useful definition.

In ITIL® we have an SKMS (Service Knowledge Management System) that contains information systems such as the AMIS (Availability Management Information System), CMIS (Capacity Management Information System and SMIS (Security Management Information System) and there are others too.

These information systems contain databases that are populated by various ITIL® processes. Getting the right information to the right people at the right time involves allowing them access (with suitable controls) to the information contained in the SKMS.

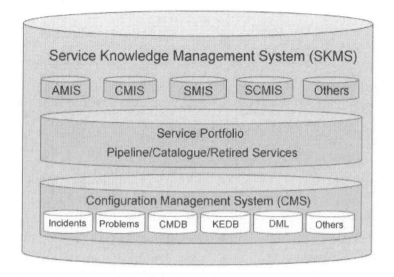

The SKMS contains Management Information Systems (MIS) including:

- CMS (Configuration Management System)
- AMIS (Availability MIS)
- CMIS (Capacity MIS)
- SMIS (Security MIS)
- SCMIS (Supplier & Contract MIS)
- Service Portfolio

Then, the Management Information Systems contain databases, for example, the CMS contains:

- Incident Database
- Problem Database
- KEDB

- CMDB

From the above, you can see that there are 3 distinct levels in the SKMS: the level of the database container, the level of the information system container and the very top-level of the knowledge container, the SKMS itself. So, we can see that the structure of the SKMS conforms to a conceptual model that you may have previously encountered in some other context i.e. the D-I-K-W Model.

- D ... Data
- I ... Information
- K ... Knowledge
- W ... Wisdom

The difference between data and information is context i.e. information is data set into context. Similarly, the difference between information and knowledge is further context. To use an analogy: data is like the words in a message, information is like a sentence and knowledge is the meaning of the whole communication.

- *60* ... This is an example of data
- *Filesystem 60% Full* ... This is information
- *We will run out of space in 30 days* ... Knowledge

Modern toolsets allow us to get the information (held within the various information systems inside the SKMS) into context so we can understand the meaning of the data we have been gathering.

The SKMS does not contain wisdom – that is the human judgement applied to the knowledge. What would it be wise to do if our filesystem was going to fill up in 30 days? Add a disk and grow the filesystem before it happens – that's wisdom.

Of course, the SKMS needs to be built and maintained and that is part of the job of this process i.e. to ensure that this is done, bearing in mind that many ITIL® processes actually populate and maintain the individual component databases and information systems.

Using suitable tools to browse, query and search the SKMS, the data held within the various databases is set into context so that it becomes meaningful information. This information can be presented in useful and understandable format, such as graphs, bar charts and so on, and by analysing that information, wise decisions can be made.

Incident Management

We briefly discussed this process as an example at the beginning when we were drawing the distinction between processes and functions. Now, here are the actual steps of the process, as defined in the guidance:

- Logging
- Categorisation
- Prioritisation
- Analysis
- Functional Escalation
- Monitoring
- Tracking
- Closing

Logging – involves recording the incident in a database

Categorisation – hardware or software; which application etc

Prioritisation – involves setting an initial priority

Analysis – is an initial attempt at resolution

Functional Escalation – getting the call to the right specialist

Monitoring/Tracking – keeping an eye on incident progress

Closing – requires confirmation from the user

During the *categorisation* activity, the Service Desk analyst is attempting to identify which specific items in the infrastructure are actually affected. This requires a certain amount of skill in decoding what is being said by the user and then matching the information against records in our CMDB. You will remember that the CMDB is one of many databases that comprise the **CMS** (Configuration Management System).

The priority of an incident is set according to two factors: **impact** and **urgency**:

- Impact … the effect on the business/operation
- Urgency … how quickly it needs to be resolved

It is possible for an incident to be high-impact (e.g. lots of users affected) but low urgency (i.e. plenty of time available to fix), just as the reverse situation – low-impact, high-urgency - is also possible.

Request Fulfilment

When people call the service desk, which is defined as the 'single point of contact for all users of IT services' they do so for all kinds of reasons.

- They need help with software
- They forgot their password
- Something is broken
- They need a new laptop
- They want to make a complaint

The best way to think of these types of demands is that they are either *incidents* or they are not. If the call is not an incident, then nothing is wrong with our services and therefore, nothing needs to be diagnosed or fixed. That type of call i.e. where nothing is wrong, is not an incident; it is a *service request*.

With service requests all we have to do is log them, track them and, subject to appropriate authorisations being in place, escalate them to the appropriate group to fulfil the request and that's exactly what this process does.

So where does a password reset fit: is it an incident or a service request? You could actually argue the toss either way and there are certainly many organisations that deal with them as incidents. There is nothing wrong with that if that is your organisation's policy.

Either way, the call gets logged and dealt with within agreed timescales, so it should not concern the user – either way – as to how the call is categorised. But personally, I would classify them as service requests simply for management information purposes. That way, our incident stats are much more meaningful and useful to roles that make use of the data including the Service Level Manager, the Incident Manager and the Problem Manager.

Note: For much more on the subject of Incident Management, please see my book <u>Incident Management for Newbies</u> which is now available in good online stores.

Problem Management

The Problem Management process is specifically responsible for adding data to the **Known Error Database** (KEDB) – a database to be found in the CMS. In particular, it is responsible for producing and documenting **workarounds**. This is a key output of the process

A second key output of this process is the production of **Requests for Change** (RFCs) to get permanent fixes initiated in the infrastructure.

Two Key Outputs

- Production of Workarounds
- Production of RFCs

Analysis techniques used by this process include **Kepner Tregoe** (a problem-solving methodology) and the use of **Ishikawa Diagrams** (a brainstorming technique).

Problem Management is involved in **Trend Analysis** – a method of identifying the existence of underlying problems. If a particular user is continually experiencing the Blue-Screen-of-Death syndrome or a particular router is continually getting into an error condition, then these are examples of trends.

The existence of a trend almost certainly implies an underlying problem and this process would be responsible for finding that cause and doing something about it i.e. producing a workaround or an RFC (or both).

The process is both reactive and proactive. Reactive Problem Management investigates underlying causes after an incident or incidents have occurred; Proactive Problem Management attempts to uncover problems that have not yet caused incidents. When a car manufacturer recalls a particular model to get a component of the steering or the brakes changed, that is an example of proactive Problem management in the real world.

Note: For much more on the subject of Problem Management, please see my book Problem Management for Newbies which is now available in good online stores.

Event Management

Imagine for a moment that you are driving along in your car and the oil light or the petrol light illuminates on the dash. Everything seems fine, the car has not stopped and indeed, performance has not been affected at all. But if you don't pull in at the next service station and do something about that warning, you are going to finish up with a service interruption.

The petrol light is not notifying you of an incident; it is notifying you that something 'significant' has changed state and it is a very good example of what we mean by an *event*. An event is defined as: a 'change of state that has significance' for a CI or a service. There are very many pieces of hardware, software and firmware that are capable of generating event messages, often in SNMP (Simple Network Management Protocol) format, that can notify us of 'significant' changes of state that have not yet caused incidents.

Often, this process is fully automated. Using programmable tools, we set our own rules (known as *correlation rules*) to specify what we want to happen when an event is detected. Of course, the relevant action will depend upon the level of significance of the event itself. Some events have a very low level of significance, for example, a user has logged on; other events, like a warning that a filesystem is nearly full (that's a bit like running out of petrol) have a much higher level of significance.

So the job of this process is to detect these events, make sense of them and then trigger the appropriate control action – whatever that happens to be.

In the case of the user logging in, the appropriate action might simply be to log the event. But with the filesystem warning, the appropriate action could be to raise an incident so as to get a human involved. With modern technology, we might go a lot further with our automated responses. Staying with the same example, we might also have a prepared disk standing by and a script that could be invoked to add it to the filesystem.

It can be a challenge to get the right tools and to program them correctly. In particular, getting the level of filtering right (some events are of such a low level of significance that they may be usefully ignored) is very important. But of course, the more you get into Event Management, the more proactive you are being.

Access Management

Access Management concerns the physical granting (and revoking) of rights and privileges so that people can gain access to the software, systems and services they need to carry out the responsibilities of their roles.

The process does not decide who can have access to what; that is a policy decision made by another process i.e. the Information Security Management process. However, this process (Access Management) may be thought of as the execution arm of security.

Ideally, we would integrate the process with the organisation's HR Function because, hopefully, they will know when we have new starters joining the company and also what their roles will be. When we are informed of that kind of information, in advance, we are able to create the various accounts and logins, and grant the necessary access rights that will be needed by those people.

Similarly, when people get promoted, demoted, or perhaps they leave the organisation, for one reason or another or, possibly, have died, access rights may need to be granted or revoked and HR is ideally placed to provide us with the necessary notifications. The same is true for contractors who work for the organisation for certain periods of time: they may need access to our systems just for those periods.

Of course, if for some reason, after starting work for us, a person does not have access to the necessary systems, they would call the Service Desk. The Service Desk would be expected to log the matter as a Service Request and escalate it to the appropriate group for fulfilment (this would involve someone in either the IT Operations Management or the Applications Management functions depending on the organisations policy).

However, before escalation, the Service Desk would check the identity of the individual and also check whether the person's role is allowed access to the requested systems. Both of these checking steps are a part of the process, along with the actual granting of rights.

7-Step Improvement Process

Earlier, we discussed the Deming Cycle (Plan, Do, Check, Act) - this could really be thought of as the philosophy that underpins the discipline of Continual Service Improvement (CSI) - and the 7 Step Improvement Process is really ITIL's ® version of it.

Here are the steps:

- What is the Vision?
- Define what will be Measured
- Gather the Data
- Process the Data
- Analyze the Information
- Present and use the Information
- Implement the Improvement

The key to understanding this process is to recognise that the activities are carried out by other parts of ITIL®.

The vision is, of course, set by Service Strategy and the 'defining what should be measured' step is carried out as part of the design of a new service i.e. at the design stage, we don't just design the service, we also design the measurement methods too; it is one of the 5 aspects of Service Design – remember?

Similarly, 'gathering the data' is done by the many processes that perform various activities and populate our databases with performance data. For example, the Incident Management process populates the Incident Database. This (together with data from many other processes) is what is being gathered as we go about our normal Business-as-Usual (BAU) operations.

When we have an SKMS in place, we have the necessary tools to crunch all of the data held in those databases and process it into information that we can present and analyse and, in that analysis, we are looking for improvement opportunities.

During analysis, we would be asking question such as these:

- Do we see any clear trends?
- Are they positive or negative?
- Are they good or bad?
- Are we operating as planned?
- Are we meeting our targets?
- Are any improvements required?

Once improvement opportunities are recognised, they get logged in the CSI Register which is also held within the SKMS. The CSI Manager, who has a budget to work within, will then select the best opportunities from the register and raise the necessary RFCs to get them implemented.

Implementing IT Service Management

It can be a bit overwhelming to read through 26 process descriptions and get your head around them and 4 functions too. The experience is something akin to trying to learn how a car works by studying all of the component parts and that's why, in this book, we looked at an overview of IT Service Management first, using Version 2 of ITIL® as grist for the mill, so to speak.

We have encountered the 4 Ps once or twice already. You may recall that there are actually two sets of 4 Ps in ITIL® - one set in Service Strategy (Perspective, Position, Plan and Patterns); the other in Service Design (People, Processes, Products and Partners). Well, the latter is a very good way of thinking about what IT Service Management is, at the top level.

IT Service Management is: *People* working with *Partners* using *Processes* embedded into *Products* (our integrated toolset). The people are divided into functions (we discussed 4 functions); partners are external organisations that play a part in the delivery of our services; products, in this context, are the tools (software) we are using to perform the processes we discussed.

In practice, the adoption of IT Service Management in any particular organisation means cherry-picking from the guidance. You don't have to adopt all of the processes and you don't have to copy the exact steps of any of the processes either. The overall message is that you should 'adapt and adopt' the guidance to the specific needs of your organisation.

In practice, your adaptation of these principles will be mixed in with practices derived from a variety of sources including your own experience and learning as well as guidance from other sources of Best Practice such as PRINCE2 (Project Management) Six Sigma (Process Improvement) COBIT (IT Service Management) and so on – there are many relevant additional frameworks you might profitably utilise.

When it comes to introducing IT Service Management into your organisation, you might decide to appoint a project manager and treat the whole thing as a project – that's certainly a good approach. However, you might instead like to think about using the CSI Approach that we encountered in the Continual Service Improvement book i.e. instead of running a project, use the ITIL® guidance as your vision and work toward it by initiating little cycles of improvement.

Here is the CSI Approach again:

- What's the Vision? ... ITIL® Can Provide it!
- Where are we now? ... A Baseline Assessment
- Where do we want to be? ... A Target
- How do we get there? ... A Plan
- Have we arrived? ... A Measurement

- How to maintain Momentum? ... Next Improvement

There is no right way to do this, except what is right for your organisation. But one way is to think in terms of processes. Start by *baselining*: which of the processes we have discussed do you actually have in place and how mature are those processes? There are process maturity frameworks that can help you decide, including the one in the appendix of the ITIL® Service Design book.

Then set yourself a measureable target; perhaps this might be to introduce a new process or to improve one of your existing processes – for example, are you doing Problem Management or Change Management as well as you might?

Use the guidance to help you with the design or redesign of the process you intend to introduce, or improve, and then produce a plan for its introduction. Make sure you involve the people who will be affected by the changes in the discussions up-front and genuinely take their ideas into account. Don't make the mistake of thinking the books must be right; they are a good source of guidance but, as we have discussed, they are not the only source.

Get your plan together and implement it whilst measuring your actual results. Tweak it if you need to (remember Plan-Do-Check-Act) – for that matter, keep tweaking it if you need to, until you get that one process to the level of maturity you require. Then stop, consolidate, drive the improvements into the organisation's working methods. And – when you are ready and not before – select another process and repeat the improvement cycle.

Always keep the vision in mind and remember to do what is right for your organisation. Don't be rigid in your interpretation of what the books say. Use ITIL® as the guidance it was intended to be – *adapt* and *adopt* the principles and processes to the needs of your organisation and you are sure to enjoy great success.

Part 2

Incident Management for Newbies

Foreword to Incident Management

Before we can realise the vision that Service Management most tantalisingly promises is possible - the kind of joined-up organisational thinking that connects a business with the technology it needs to achieve its vision - it is first necessary to have a good holistic view of Service Management and how its various component parts contribute to the overall goal.

When we are considering a process like Incident Management, we therefore need to understand, not only what it is and how it operates, but how it fits into the grand scheme of things. That is why, in this book, we will consider, not only the Incident Management process, but also how it fits in with Service Management functions and how it supports, and is supported by, other Service Management processes.

This book and others in this series may be used to acquire or deepen your understanding of the Service Management discipline. It is also a very useful study aid for readers who are preparing to take the ITIL® Foundation Examination.

Introduction to Incident Management

When adopting best practice guidance for Service Management, many organisations choose to begin their campaigns by addressing their Service Desk and operational processes. As the value to the business of operational processes such as Incident Management is very easy to appreciate, the reasons are understandable.

Whilst service outages are sometimes inevitable, having an efficient and effective Incident Management process in place translates to less downtime and reduced business disruption and the cost savings leveraged by improving Incident Management, therefore, are often more than enough to justify the effort. Greater levels of efficiency and effectiveness can be achieved when Incident Management is properly integrated with other operational processes such as Problem Management and Event Management.

As further areas of Service Management are adopted, transitional processes such as Knowledge Management and Service Asset & Configuration Management improve an organisation's ability to handle service outages by facilitating the business of getting information to the right person, at the right time so that the right decisions can be made much more swiftly.

Gradually, as the adoption Service Management is further embraced, new services begin to enter their operational phase with *serviceability* (3rd party recoverability) and *maintainability* (ease of recovery) actually built in to their design, further enhancing the efficiency of Incident Management. As business-focussed strategies are implemented, and a philosophy of continuous improvement is adopted, ever better alignment of IT activity with business priorities, delivering better services that meet or exceed business requirements is the natural result.

ITIL® & Incident Management

The ITIL® framework of Best Practice for IT Service Management from the OGC (Office of Government Commerce) consists of a set of five volumes which together make up what has become known as the *core guidance*.

Here is a list of the Official ITIL® publications in the core guidance:

- Service Strategy (SS)
- Service Design (SD)
- Service Transition (ST)
- Service Operation (SO)
- Continual Service Improvement (CSI)

Just from the titles, you can see that the structure of the guidance follows the *lifecycle* of a service all the way from concept, through design, build, test and into the live environment where it gets continually improved until it is eventually retired.

At a top level, here's what each of those volumes are concerned with:

Service Strategy

This book is about the future and, in particular, it is about the future of the portfolio of services offered by the service provider. The guidance concerns top level business thinking around strategic direction, and effectively managing the portfolio so as to achieve the business strategy, expressed in terms of plans, policies, and vision.

Here are the processes described in Service Strategy:

- Strategy Management for IT Services
- Financial Management for IT Services
- Service Portfolio Management
- Demand Management
- Business Relationship Management

Service Design

The guidance in this book concerns the design of services, naturally, but it is also concerned with the design of other aspects of Service Management such as processes, metrics, architectures and tools. Service Design translates the requirements of the organisation into a package of plans and specifications and then hands them over to the next phase of the lifecycle.

Here are the processes included in Service Design:

- Design Coordination
- Capacity Management
- IT Service Continuity Management (ITSCM)
- Availability Management
- Service Catalogue Management
- Information Security management
- Service Level Management
- Supplier Management

Service Transition

This book deals with checking and executing the plans prepared by the previous phase (Service Design) so that a new (or significantly changed) service is gracefully introduced (built, tested and deployed) into the live environment when it is handed over to the next phase of the lifecycle for ongoing support. The central theme of this book concerns the protection of the live environment i.e. ensuring that the introduction of significant changes do not adversely affect the business.

Here are the processes in Service Transition:

- Transition Planning
- Release & Deployment Management
- Change Evaluation
- Service Validation & Testing
- Service Asset & Configuration Management
- Change Management
- Knowledge Management

Service Operation

This book is about the ongoing support of services that are already deployed within the live environment. The guidance concerns both the handling of service interruptions and also dealing with various other types of request made by users. In addition, there is guidance on proactive activities designed to reduce service outages and eliminate their causes.

Here are the processes discussed in Service Operation:

- Problem Management

- Incident Management
- Request Fulfilment
- Event Management
- Access Management

Continual Service Improvement

The Continual Service Improvement (CSI) volume concerns the improvement not only of services but of every aspect of Service Management including processes, entire lifecycle phases and Service Management as a whole. Embracing the thinking of William Edwards Deming, the guidance deals with the delivery of measureable, incremental improvements that move the service provider in the direction of the strategic vision.

Here is the single process included in CSI:

- 7-Step Improvement Process

From the foregoing, we can see that Incident Management is a process defined within the Service Operation volume of the ITIL® core guidance. More specifically, Incident Management is the process that is responsible for dealing with service interruptions and any degradation of service that adversely affects users.

This book provides a comprehensive introduction to the Incident Management process. In addition, we look at a number of related operational processes (Request Fulfilment, Event Management and Problem Management) in some detail and we also consider the responsibilities of the Service Desk.

For readers who require a comprehensive introduction to ITIL® and IT Service Management as a whole, please see my book <u>IT Service Management for Newbies</u> which is now available on the Kindle platform.

Some Important Terms

As the stated goal of the ITIL® Incident Management process is the 'restoration of normal service as soon as possible' perhaps a good place to start is by considering what exactly constitutes a service, what is meant by the phrase 'normal service' and what exactly is an incident.

In a nutshell, services are intangible entities that sit in between business processes and IT architecture.

Business processes, as distinct from Service Management processes, are what the organisation is actually doing to provide value to its customers. In the case of a garage, business processes might include *servicing*, *MOT certification* and *breakdown recovery*; for a training company, business processes might include *course delivery*, *consultancy* and *training needs evaluation*.

Some business processes might be absolutely unique to a particular organisation though many business processes are likely to be quite similar to those of other companies that operate within the same market spaces. But whatever it is that your business actually does can be described as a process. As the great William Edwards Deming once said, "If you can't describe what you are doing as a process, you don't know what you are doing!"

It really is not that long ago that companies operated entirely without the aid of computers. Although there were notable forerunners, the first machine we would recognise as a programmable computer was invented during World War II and the first significant wave of computerisation, within business, occurred as recently as the nineteen eighties at around the time of the launch of the IBM® PC.

These days, it is very difficult to imagine modern businesses operating without IT. The fact is that many of our business processes are entirely dependent, or partly dependent, upon IT in some way and this is the accepted scenario within which modern businesses now operate. Most businesses (or organisations) are heavily dependent upon IT and the whole reason IT exists within those operations is to enable the business to achieve its goals and mission.

The situation poses a couple of interesting questions:

- How can IT provide the infrastructure and systems the business (organisation) requires if it does not fully understand the business processes, goals and mission?

- How can those responsible for executing business processes and moving the organisation in the direction of its goals effectively and meaningfully interact with IT staff, given the increasingly complex IT architecture that most businesses now have in place?

The fact is that, in most organisations, IT does not fully understand the business and the reverse is also true i.e. that the business does not fully understand IT. This state of affairs is sometimes referred to as the *knowledge gap* and bridging the knowledge gap is what IT Service Management is all about. That is why we **choose** to define what we provide to the business as *services* and not as IT infrastructure and applications software.

So this is the basic idea to bear in mind ...

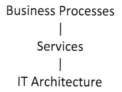

Business Processes
|
Services
|
IT Architecture

N.B IT architecture consists of the necessary software, infrastructure, data and environment.

As we noted, above, services are the intangible entities that sit in between business processes and IT architecture. They consist of the individual items of hardware, software (and anything else that is a component part of the service) and they underpin business processes. As an example, think of the *email service* that your company almost certainly has in place. It consists of the individual elements of IT architecture (server, clients, network, gateway, software etc) and it underpins many diverse business processes.

Already, you may begin to see some of the advantages of defining the above collection of items as a service. The average business user has no idea what an X400/SMTP Gateway is, or what it does, but they do understand what email is - talking in the language of services, rather than the language of IT, is very helpful middle ground.

So, you see, your organisation's services are indeed intangible things and, if your business decides to implement IT Service Management, *your* services will need to be defined. That is what the Service Catalogue Management process within ITIL® actually does. A good service catalogue will not simply be a list of services; it will actually contain all of the details we have been discussing i.e. what items the services consist of (technically known as *configuration items* in ITIL®) and which business processes they underpin.

Now that we know what a service is, we need to consider what is meant by the phrase 'normal service' and this is quite straightforward. Normal service is, quite simply, whatever has been defined and agreed in the Service Level Agreement (SLA). The SLA is a written agreement we have in place with our customer(s) and in that agreement, we describe exactly what the customer is expected to receive so there should be absolutely no uncertainty or ambiguity.

At a top-level, here are the typical contents of an SLA:

- Dates (Start Date, End Date, Review Date)
- Parties to the Agreement
- Signatories
- Brief Description of the Services Provided
- Service Level Targets
- Responsibilities (User and Service Provider)

Service Level Agreements are negotiated, documented, agreed and regularly reviewed by the Service Level Management process in ITIL®.

Finally, we need to discuss what we mean by the term *incident*. Here is the definition from the official ITIL® Glossary …

> *An unplanned interruption to an IT service or reduction in the quality of an IT service.*

From the above, we can see that when we have a service that is interrupted or reduced in quality, then we have an incident. When it comes to the degradation of a service, the SLA is an important reference. The document is meant to remove any potential ambiguity over perceived performance because it should specify, in terms the user can understand (such as transaction turn-around times) exactly what level of service the customer can expect to receive.

It may possibly surprise you to learn that some failures that do not apparently affect the service (such as the failure of a disk in a mirrored set) are also considered to be incidents. Even though users may perceive no degradation to services that are using the disk (in this example) the service *is* actually degraded because its resilience has been impacted.

Our services are the product of two entities: *utility* and *warranty*. Utility is what the service actually does; in other words, its functionality. Warranty is a kind of guarantee and in ITIL®, there are actually four parts to the guarantee.

Warranty is a product of:

- Availability
- Capacity
- Security
- Continuity

The guarantee is that the service will be there when it is needed (availability); we won't run out as demand increases (capacity); it will be secure enough (security) to be usable; and it will be fully recoverable (continuity).

Any failure that impacts any of those four areas affects the guarantee (warranty) of the service and so is, rightly, treated as an incident.

Who is the Customer?

ITIL® began in the UK as a means of distilling best practice from excellent organisations operating as service providers in the real world. The original idea was to define terms, processes and methods for the benefit of the UK public sector and the original books, therefore, were written assuming that the service provider was providing services to an internal organisation.

As time moved on, ITIL® guidance was embraced by many organisations which were operating within the private sector, providing services to external customers. Although much of the original guidance was relevant to such businesses, it became clear that the public sector was no longer the exclusive target audience for the guidance. So, in recent years, more effort has been made to ensure the books are more generic and it is worth bearing in mind that there are three different service provider types at whom the present books are aimed.

Service Provider Types:

- Type 1 ... a Type 1 service provider supports a single internal customer (business unit).

- Type 2 ... a Type 2 provider that supports multiple internal customers (business units).

- Type 3 ... a Type 3 service provider supports external customers.

As you can see from the above, the key differentiation is to be found in who the provider is setup to serve, not whether or not the service provider is operating in the public sector. When ITIL® refers to 'the business' therefore, it means the top level of the organisation i.e. that unit of the organisation that benefits from the use of the services provided.

A *business unit* is a part of the organisation that has its own vision, plans, costs and income. If your service operation serves a single, internal business unit (whether you operate in the public or private sectors) that makes you a type 1 service provider. If your service operation serves multiple, internal business units, that makes you a type 2 provider.

To illustrate the difference between type 1 and type 2: here in the UK a number of years back, it was common for each of the district health authorities operating within the NHS (National Health Service) to have their own IT departments. With that arrangement, each of those IT departments served only one customer organisation i.e. a single business unit, so they were all type 1 service providers. In recent years, in order to leverage economies of scale, the arrangement has changed to type 2 where they now have a service operation (technically known as a *shared services unit*) providing IT to multiple district authorities.

If your organisation markets a catalogue of services to external customers, then that distinction makes you a type 3 provider. Of course, it is perfectly possible that your own service organisation might serve both internal and external customers. If that were the case, consider the main purpose of your existence as a service provider because there is likely to be a central focus. Essentially, identifying your service provider type all boils down to answering the question: who is, or who are, our customer(s)?

When a provider is not charging for the services it provides (as *may* be the case with type 1 or 2 service providers), staff can struggle with the idea of thinking about the people they serve as actually being customers. When working with public sector clients, I do sometimes hear the objection "but we don't have customers." However, this is really a matter of mind-set because, whether or not people pay for the services they receive, we can indeed think of them and treat them as customers.

Where the ITIL® guidance deals with issues such as creating *differentiated offerings* in order to stimulate sales, again, it may at first seem to be not entirely relevant to service providers that don't charge. But that is really not the case; such apparently commercially focussed areas of the guidance (a central theme of the Service Strategy volume) is highly relevant to providers that don't charge because they still need to be able to benchmark themselves against commercial alternatives and demonstrate a competitive edge to the business – or potentially face the prospect of being outsourced.

As you can see, by drawing the distinctions between service provider types, the guidance has now, effectively, abstracted itself from its public sector roots and the basic idea is that it should continue to be relevant to *both* the public and private sectors. This is an important point because, as you will now understand from the foregoing, interpretation of the guidance will be subtly different for public and private sector organisations.

One way or another, our customers can and do exercise choice even in situations where this may not be entirely evident. The important thing is to always bear in mind that we, as service providers, are there to serve our customers whether they are internal or external and whether or not they are paying for the services we provide. This is one of the most important things to get across to Service Desk staff.

Functions

In ITIL® the Service Desk is defined as a *function* and so we need to be clear about what that means.

Quite simply, a function consists of the people and tools used to execute one or more processes. By the way, the term 'Service Desk', rather than 'Help Desk', is a much better description of what this function is about, after all, we are service providers, the overall discipline is called Service Management and we are concerned with service related issues (interruptions and degradation).

The Service Desk is not the only function described in ITIL® and is not the only one active within your organisation. There are functions that sit outside of Service Management, such as Human Resources, Marketing, Sales, Research & Development and so on, and there are functions within Service Management including the Service Desk. Other Service Management functions described in ITIL® include IT Operations Management, Technical Management and Applications Management.

The distinction between functions and processes is essentially the difference between *who* and *what*.

- Process: *what* is being done
- Function: *who* is doing it

In practice, you can have as many functions within your Service Management capability as your organisation requires. Sometimes, the activities of a particular process might become so important to an organisation that people and tools become dedicated to that particular process. For example, Capacity Management (whilst it appears in the Service Design book as a process) <u>could</u>, within your organisation, be designated as a function if you were to have a group of people, with the necessary tools, dedicated to performing it.

For the ITIL® Foundation examination, you need to have a basic understanding of what the following four Service Management functions do …

Service Desk

The Service Desk is the 'single point of contact for all users of IT services'. It doesn't matter who is calling or what they want, if they need to interact with IT, they should call the Service Desk – that's what it means to be a *single point of contact*. The Service Desk will log the issue, whatever it happens to be, and deal with it in the appropriate manner.

Technical Management

Technical Management is the function responsible for the *infrastructure*. It provides knowledge, guidance and the actual resources (people, tools, equipment) for the maintenance of the infrastructure. The people in this function are our subject matter experts in the area of infrastructure.

Whenever technical expertise, in the area of <u>infrastructure</u>, is required, by ITIL® processes, this function provides the necessary expertise.

Main responsibilities include the following:

- Skills Inventories & Documentation
- Training Programs
- Recruiting/Contracting Resources
- Definition of Organisation's Standards
- Design of Services
- Active in Various Processes

Application Management

Application Management is the function responsible for *application software*. It provides knowledge, guidance and the actual resources for the maintenance of applications. It is also the interface to the software development environment. Again, these people are subject matter experts, but in the area of software.

Whenever technical expertise, in the area of <u>applications software</u>, is required, by ITIL® processes, this function provides the necessary expertise.

Main responsibilities include the following:

- Skills Inventories & Documentation
- Training Programs
- Recruiting/Contracting Resources
- Definition of Organisation's Standards
- Design of Services
- Active in Various Processes

IT Operations Management

IT Operations Management is the function responsible for general 'housekeeping' activities such as managing print jobs, backup, job scheduling, monitoring and so on. The collective ITIL® term for such housekeeping is *Operations Control*. People in this function generally have a wide range of technical skills including both hardware and software expertise.

Note that, in many organisations, *Facilities Management* will be a separate function however, it is described as a responsibility of the *IT Operations Management* function in the ITIL® guidance. In relation to the physical environment, *Facilities Management* includes the management of:

- Datacentres/Buildings
- Equipment Hosting
- Power Supplies
- Environment
- Personal Safety
- Physical Access
- Goods in/out
- Building Maintenance

Tip: For the ITIL® Foundation Exam, remember that *Facilities Management* and *Operations Control* (with all they entail) are responsibilities of the *IT Operations Management* function.

Personnel from all of the above functions might be involved in the Incident Management process.

Often, in addition to logging and prioritising incidents, the Service Desk will provide first line support, the IT Operations Management function might provide second line support and the Technical and Applications Management functions could provide third line support. Of course, that might not strictly be the case because you can have first, second and third line support provided by whichever group(s) you, as a service provider choose to designate. For example, you might outsource third line support to an external specialist organisation – this is not an uncommon choice.

Whichever groups – internal and/or external – are involved in Incident Management, the Service Desk will ensure that calls are escalated to the appropriate group at the right time – this is known as *functional escalation* in ITIL®. However, the Service Desk will retain ownership of all incidents and so ensure that the progress of calls is monitored and tracked, and that they are eventually closed.

So as we can see, having a good Service Desk in place is a very important component of an effective Incident Management process or, as we would say using ITIL® language, it is a *critical success factor* (CSF).

The Service Desk

The benefits to your organisation of having a good Service Desk really cannot be overstated. Some of the more important benefits include improving customer satisfaction and retention, maintaining proper focus on the business goals and assisting in identifying service improvements.

Despite the fact that the Service Desk is such an important function and, to a very large extent, influences how IT is perceived within an organisation, it is one of the most common functions for businesses to outsource. Of course, it is ultimately for each individual business to decide whether or not to outsource, but the decision should not be taken lightly.

There are a number of issues of which to be aware when outsourcing.

> Firstly, the external service provider should use compatible tools and processes, so that the management of your services continues to flow seamlessly across the organisational divide.

> Secondly, there needs to be very good communication between the outsourced desk and any other groups involved in the provision of support.

> Thirdly, it is imperative that the important support documents we have discussed (SLAs. OLAs and Contracts) are properly negotiated, agreed and signed off.

Finally, you must ensure that the ownership of all data collected by the outsourced desk in relation to *your* customers, configurations, incidents and so on remains the property of your company. This is essential, as some organisations have found out, to their cost, when attempting to subsequently reverse their decision to outsource.

Any potential cost savings should be weighed against possible reductions in customer satisfaction and consequential business impacts should the function be subsequently handled badly as a result of outsourcing. That is not to say that a reduction in quality would necessarily follow, just that the business should be clear about exactly how the customer experience might be affected by the decision.

Service Desk Structures

There are three specific types (or structures) of Service Desk mentioned in ITIL®; they are known as *local*, *central* and *virtual*.

Supposing that an organisation had offices located in three different centres which are geographically spread throughout the country. One option for the service provider is to put a Service Desk in each physical location – that is what is meant by a *local* Service Desk. An alternative arrangement would be to have a single Service Desk that serves the entire organisation – that would be a *central* Service Desk.

Comparing and contrasting the local and central Service Desks, there are advantages and disadvantages to both of these arrangements.

- Local Desk ... Serves a Single Physical Location
- Central Desk ... Serves the Entire Operation

Advantages of a local desk include: better access (easier and quicker) to affected equipment, software and systems, local knowledge, understanding of local culture, language, dialect etc. However, this arrangement is usually more costly to run and managing and monitoring local desks can be more complex especially where data, information and knowledge needs to be passed between them. This is an important consideration when you think of the implications of synchronising incident and problem data or maintaining a centralised recording system.

There are many advantages to the central desk arrangement which flow from the economies of scale to be leveraged. These advantages include: reductions in operating costs, optimising use of shared resources and simplifying management and monitoring activities. Of course, the trade-off is that the advantages of the local desk are typically lost.

A third option is to have Service Desk personnel geographically distributed across the various centres but to connect them via telephony. In this arrangement, there is still a single point of contact that serves the entire operation even though the staff are not located in a single physical location – that is what is meant by a *virtual* Service Desk.

- Virtual Desk ... Serves the Entire Operation but Staff are Not Located at a Single Physical Site

The advantages of the virtual desk encompass those of both the central and local desk arrangements, and a well organised desk can truly provide the best of both worlds. Of course, to facilitate this arrangement, you would need special telephony for routing calls efficiently across different physical locations and you would also need high speed communication links to a centralised datacentre at which your SKMS (Service Knowledge Management System) would be located.

Here is a simplified representation of the SKMS ...

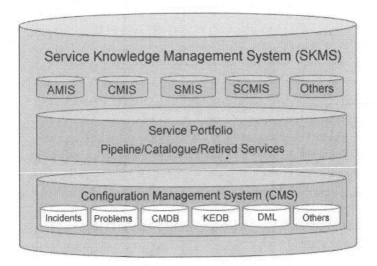

As you can see, the CMS (Configuration Management System), which is extensively utilised by Service Desk personnel is an important part of the SKMS.

The incident database holds incident records that are raised and subsequently updated during the progress of incidents and problems. This activity is usually carried out by Service Desk staff. Problem records are usually raised and updated by the Problem Manager however, Service Desk staff will refer recurring incidents to the Problem Management process for consideration because recurring incidents are one way of identifying the existence of problems (more about this later).

The CMDB (Configuration Management Database) contains details of the individual items (configuration items) that make up the services and this information is frequently interrogated (and may also be updated) by Service Desk staff during the process of incident management. The KEDB (Known Error Database) is also frequently interrogated (but not updated) during Incident Management as it is the central repository for *workarounds* (temporary fixes) that may be passed on to users by the Service Desk.

Note: Updating of the KEDB i.e. populating and updating it with new *workarounds* is actually carried out by the Problem Management process.

The Skill Set

Some organisations use call loggers (non-technical staff) to answer the telephone, raise incident records and then escalate the incidents to more specialist staff – this is sometimes known as an *unskilled* desk. Others actually put technical specialists on the Service Desk with the intention of logging and dealing with as many incidents as possible, as they arrive – this is an *expert* desk. Still others utilise staff who have broad, but limited, technical ability to log and deal with the most common incidents as they arrive – this sometimes called a *skilled* desk.

- Unskilled Desk ... Uses Call Loggers
- Skilled Desk ... Some Technical Expertise
- Expert Desk ... Uses Technical Specialists

Note: The terms *unskilled*, *skilled* and *expert* do not appear in the ITIL guidance after Version 2, though the principle does.

Which of these options is right for your service organisation is something you need to carefully consider. There is the obvious trade-off i.e. that direct access to technical specialists *may* result in better service however, they are usually more expensive for the company to provide. But, there is a less obvious trade-off to be considered, the roots of which are to be found in the way that individuals have unconsciously 'wired' their brains.

The fact is that some people are very good at logical analysis and problem-solving. They have developed the kind of skills that are very useful for resolving incidents and problems. Other people have internalised the kind of habits (such as a natural tendency to empathise with other people) that make them very good at dealing with people. Ideally, you would want to select people who are good at both. But, in practice, you will often have to make a choice and many organisations prefer to employ staff who possess good customer skills for Service Desk roles though, thankfully, both sets of skills can be learned i.e. you can learn how to think analytically and you can also learn how to deal with people.

Here is a list of skills you should be looking for when recruiting Service Desk staff:

- Customer Focussed
- Articulate
- Good Interpersonal Skills
- Understanding of Business
- Methodical/Analytical

- Technical Knowledge
- [Multi-Lingual]

- Being customer-focused means putting customer satisfaction at the top of the agenda.

- Being articulate is having a good command of the language.

- Having good interpersonal skills means being able to deal with people effectively

- Having an understanding of the business means appreciating how the business perspective differs from the technical view

- Being methodical and analytical means having the ability to tackle unfamiliar issues in a logical manner

- Having technical knowledge means developing the right level of specialist skills

Additional languages, of course, may or may not be required depending upon the geographical distribution of your organisation's customer base. Remember too that the level of technical skills actually required will be as is appropriate to your preference of *unskilled*, *skilled* or *expert* desk.

Is it possible for an analyst to provide the right answer to a customer, but in the wrong way, and so upset the customer in the process? Is it possible for the reverse to happen i.e. that the customer does not get the answer they require at first point of contact, but is nevertheless dealt with so skilfully that they are left feeling satisfied with the interaction?

You will recognise that the answer to both of the above questions is 'yes'.

Perhaps you may be able to recall times when the way you were dealt with, especially when a company was at fault in some way, made all the difference as to how you felt about the company, and whether or not they subsequently managed to retain your business. It is often not making a mistake that costs a company business, but the way that mistakes are subsequently handled by their service personnel.

To recruit staff that have a mixture of the above skills, and to commit to developing the skills of your existing staff, is to invest in the success of your service operation in a way that can clearly differentiate your business from the competition. This can bring about many benefits in terms of winning new customers as well as retaining existing ones.

It is an easy enough thing to understand, but it is not so easy to do in practice. As leading management consultant Peter Drucker once said,

Far too many people - especially people with great expertise in one area - are contemptuous of knowledge in other areas or believe that being bright is a substitute for knowledge. First-rate engineers, for instance, tend to take pride in not knowing anything about people. Human resource professionals, by contrast, often pride themselves on their ignorance of elementary accounting. But taking pride in such ignorance is self-defeating.

Dealing with people effectively requires that individuals gain an understanding of their own personality type and how personalities, communication styles, attitudes and body language affects other people. Once such an understanding is developed, it then becomes possible to develop the behavioural habits that make all the difference in human interaction. As Stephen Covey points out in his book, *The 7 Habits of Highly Effective People*, for individuals to gain such ability requires three things: knowledge, skill and attitude.

- Knowledge – what to do
- The Skills – how to do it
- Attitude – want to do it

With any of those components missing, people simply cannot develop. They cannot write the new behavioural scripts that they need to acquire in order to deal with people more effectively. But if people have the right attitude, if they first *want to* learn, then it becomes a matter of identifying what kind of behaviour can make the difference, and then working hard to develop the ability to use it skilfully.

It is a simple fact that misunderstanding in verbal communication is commonplace. Recognising and accepting this fact is important because the desire to improve our ability to understand, and be understood, is often enough motivation for people to engage in the difficult process of personal change.

Here is a short, but useful list of 'people skills' that good customer-facing staff should work on developing:

- Active Listening
- Paraphrasing
- Feedback
- Speaking Tone

- Body Language
- Empathy

Active listening is essentially, listening with the intention of *understanding*. You may think that this is the natural state of affairs, but in fact, very often, people are instead listening with the intention of *replying*. It is a skill that is allied to the use of both *paraphrasing* and *feedback.*

Paraphrasing is making the effort to speak in the language of the target audience i.e. to deliberately change how you use language to adopt the preferences of the person with whom you are communicating, specifically with the aim of improving the clarity of your message. Of course, you learn these preferences by actively listening to how ideas are expressed by the other party. Bearing in mind the NLP (Neuro-Linguistic Programming) principle of always being prepared to change your approach in order to achieve your goal, paraphrasing is a very powerful speaking tool.

Feedback can be used in two ways. Firstly, you can feedback your understanding of what the other person has said, specifically to give them the opportunity to *confirm* or *correct* your understanding. Secondly, you can ask the other person involved in the discussion to summarise what has been said. This gives you an opportunity to detect any misunderstanding that has passed in the opposite direction. Given that misunderstanding occurs so frequently in verbal communication, this technique is also a very powerful tool.

You need to be very careful to not sound patronising when you ask another person to summarise. This can be done effectively by ensuring you get the right tone into your voice. You should always be very careful with your voice tone because it has the power to completely change the meaning of what you say. As Tony Robbins once said,

When my mother used to call me Anthony [in her serious tone], I knew that it meant more than just my name!

In fact, it is generally accepted that about 80% of the meaning of a communication made via the telephone is conveyed in the tone of your voice (Albert Mehrabian PhD UCLA Study).

Body Language is a huge subject in its own right, but learning and making effective use of such techniques can dramatically improve your ability to develop rapport in face-to-face situations.

In particular, using the right amount of eye-contact is a very powerful tool. Making eye-contact, whilst you are speaking, subconsciously communicates openness, honesty and integrity, whilst avoiding eye-contact communicates the reverse. Though there is a lot more to it, endeavour to look into the other person's eyes for about one third of the time you are speaking – that's about right for most situations.

Finally empathy is a very powerful tool for defusing emotion and is useful whenever you are dealing with anyone who is in an unhelpful state of mind. Essentially the message you are trying to communicate is that you understand their position – even if you don't agree with it. But, it is not an easy skill to acquire because the message is generally not communicated in words, but through body-language, tone of voice and attitude.

Incident Management Process

Incident Management is the process responsible for logging all incidents and getting them to the right person so that the appropriate action can be taken whilst, at the same time, monitoring and tracking progress and then eventually closing them.

Here is an example Incident Management process ...

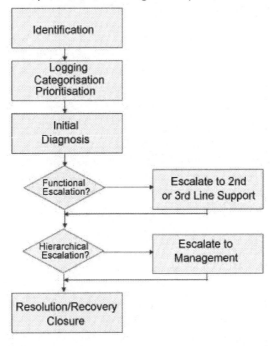

Identification – detection of the incident

Logging – recording incident details in the incident database (within the CMS)

Categorisation – identifying the type of incident

Prioritisation – setting the initial priority

Initial Diagnosis – first line analysis (and resolution wherever possible)

Escalation – getting the call to the right person

Resolution/Recovery – implementing and testing the fix

Closing – closing the incident record

Let's take a closer look at each of those steps …

Identification is the recognition that an incident has occurred. Notification can come from a human (supplier, technician or user) of course, but it might also come from an automated source such as our deployed monitoring tools.

Logging is the activity that records the details of the incident. This often (but not always) involves Service Desk staff speaking with users who are reporting something unusual or abnormal about a service they are using. Typical details recorded would include: the date and time the incident is reported, contact details for the person reporting the incident and the symptoms being experienced. Incidents are recorded in the Incident Database, one of the many databases within the CMS (Configuration Management System) which, itself, resides within the SKMS (Service Knowledge Management System).

Sometimes, incidents may reported by technical staff before users have noticed any degradation of service. In such cases, an incident record is still raised and the process operates in much the same way.

A third possibility is that an incident might be raised automatically by our Event Management tools. An **event** is not an incident; it is a 'change of state' that has some significance for a service.

Here are some examples of common events:

- A User has Logged in
- A Service is Started or Stopped
- A Warning Message is Displayed

As you can see from the above examples, not all events signify that anything unusual has happened. Users, login and out all of the time as part of normal systems operation, for example.

Each of the above examples has a different level of significance for us as service providers and some events have a level of significance which is such that human action would be typically required in order to prevent a subsequent incident from occurring. For example, supposing the warning message was announcing that a file system was 90% full. In situations like this, the Event Management tools might be programmed to automatically raise an incident record.

Categorisation is the activity that permits escalation to be carried out effectively so that incidents are correctly routed to the appropriate specialist(s) whenever necessary. It is also an important activity for the subsequent management of information, for example, when Problem Management makes use of incident data for trend analysis.

Most modern toolsets for Service Management incorporate a multi-level categorisation facility, allowing the analyst to select suitable options from drop-down boxes. Such tools are usually configurable so that the actual categories in use will be relevant for the organisation. A top level categorisation could be as simple as hardware/software and then, within each of those broad categories, we would have sub-categories as appropriate.

Categorisation Example

> Software
> Application
>   Accounting Suite
>   Nominal Ledger
>
> Hardware
> Network
> Router
>   Firmware

It is easy to see why categorisation is important for the escalation of incidents. Once we know that an incident relates to the Nominal Ledger, for example, we immediately know the correct support group to which to route the call.

Note: The *Technical Management* function defines <u>hardware</u> categories; the *Applications Management* function defines <u>software</u> categories.

Of course, this is all very well in theory. But in practice, it can be much more challenging because we typically have a user speaking with the Service Desk analyst during this step of the process. The analyst is trying to understand the reported symptoms and translate what the user is saying into an accurate assessment of which application or hardware component is affected. It is a difficult analytical skill to acquire and therefore, calls do sometimes get initially miscategorised. That is why there is often a closure category, as well as an initial category, on incident records i.e. so that processes that make use of incident data (for example, Problem Management) do have an accurate categorisation for every incident with which to work.

Of course, as we get better at Incident Management, so we should be getting better at the categorisation activity and, specifically because it is a difficult activity for service desk staff to always get right, a metric based on categorisation would make an excellent KPI (Key Performance Indicator). For example, the percentage of calls correctly categorised at first point of contact would make an excellent KPI for this process.

There are likely to be a number of incidents reported each day and so there needs to be some way for deciding which ones to tackle first and this is the purpose of the prioritisation activity. The usual factors to take into consideration in assessing and deciding upon an individual incident's priority are *impact* and *urgency*.

Factors for Assessing Priority

Impact: the effect on the business

Urgency: how long we have got to fix it

Often, the number of users affected is a good measure of impact. But impact could just as easily be measured in other ways, such as financially or simply by considering who is placing the call – some organisations use the concept of VIPs (Very Important People). So the rules for assessing impact are something the organisation itself needs to decide upon and publish in clear guidance to be issued to Service Desk staff.

Urgency is a little more straight-forward, especially if we have SLAs (Service Level Agreements) in place with our customers, because resolution times will be clearly documented and agreed, in advance, within those documents. The overall priority for an incident can then be assessed by considering a combination of these factors and then typically set as critical, high, medium or low.

During the analysis (Initial Diagnosis) step, Service Desk staff will be using their own analysis skills and also making extensive use of diagnostic scripts and information from the CMDB (Configuration Management Databases) and KEDB (Known Error Database) databases. Working in this way, some incidents will be resolved at first point of contact, whilst the user is still on the telephone.

Tip: Again, the percentage of calls resolved at first point of contact would make an excellent KPI for this process.

Many organisations allow Service Desk staff to continue to work on incidents that cannot be immediately resolved, for a limited period of time. But when that time has elapsed or when it becomes clear that the call cannot be resolved by Service

Desk staff, then the incident needs to be escalated to the appropriate, second line group.

The second line team will effectively have the same arrangement in place i.e. a limited, specified amount of time to resolve or further escalate the incident to third line support – passing the incident, in this way, is known as *functional escalation* in ITIL®. The amount of time that each of these support teams have to work with should be clearly documented in OLA (Operational Level Agreement) and/or UC (Underpinning Contract) documents.

Important Support Documents

OLA: An internal agreement between support groups
UC: An external agreement between support groups

If second line support is being provided internally, then an OLA should be negotiated and agreed. In this case, it would be an agreement between first line and second line support detailing the escalation procedure and timescales for incident resolution. Similarly, if third line support is also being provided internally, then another OLA should be negotiated and agreed between second line and third line support.

If either of these capabilities (2nd or 3rd line support) is being provided externally, then an underpinning contract should be negotiated with the external organisation again detailing the escalation procedure and timescales for incident resolution.

Whilst it is probably impossible to ensure that our SLAs (Service Level Agreements) are never breached, the basic idea of these important support documents is to minimise the chances of it happening.

A second type of escalation can occur when it becomes necessary, for whatever reason, to refer an incident higher up the management chain. It may be that a user is dissatisfied and asks to speak to a manager, or it may be that the organisation's own policy is to involve more senior staff when a particular set of criteria is met, for example, when an incident is taking too long to resolve. This type of escalation is known as *hierarchical escalation* in ITIL®.

Escalating an incident to a manager via hierarchical escalation will, of course, not interrupt the normal progress of investigation and resolution i.e. investigation will not normally cease pending some action to be taken by the manager. However, as a result of being involved, the manager may be able to allocate additional resources to assist and speed up resolution.

The Resolution and Recovery step includes the application of the fix (whatever that may involve) and subsequent testing before handing back the affected service in a fully recovered state. Whatever the fix turns out to be, it is of course, fully documented within the incident record for future reference. If restoring the service requires something to be changed, the necessary RFC (Request for Change) would be raised. This ensures that the change not only happens but also that details of the change are recorded in the CMDB (Configuration Management Database).

After taking the necessary recovery actions, the specialist team will notify the Service Desk so that the incident can then be closed.

It is worth noting that the Service Desk always 'owns' the incident, even after it is escalated. This means that the Service Desk will effectively monitor and track incident progress during its lifecycle. In addition, Service Desk staff will ensure that the incident record always gets updated wherever necessary, for example, if more information becomes available or if priorities should change during the life of the incident.

Tip: Do not get confused between the ownership of an *incident* and the ownership of a *process*. The Service Desk owns incidents. However, the Incident Management process will be owned by the relevant process owner; typically the Incident Manager.

In closing an incident, Service Desk staff will check with the user(s) that they are happy for the reported incident to be closed. This brings up the question of what to do when we believe the incident is indeed resolved, but we cannot contact the user for some reason. There are various ways to tackle this: you could automatically close such incidents after a set time has elapsed or you could operate a *three-strikes-and-you're-out* policy where you would attempt to contact the user three times and then close the incident even if the user cannot not be contacted. Whichever method is selected, it would be documented within the SLA (Service Level Agreement) so that users are aware.

During the incident closure step, the Service Desk staff have a final opportunity to check and update the incident record to ensure it is accurate. If there is a closure category field in the incident record, it would be updated at this time. Often, Service Desk staff will not appreciate the reason for this activity since the incident has, of course, been resolved by this stage. However, incident data is utilised by other Service Management processes such as Problem Management, so it is important that it is accurate. It is therefore prudent to impress the importance of this activity upon the staff responsible for updating and closing incident records.

Immediately following the closure of an incident is an ideal time to conduct a customer satisfaction check by canvassing the opinions of a selected sample.

Procedures and Models

It is often beneficial to have some pre-agreed strategy for dealing with major incidents. In practice, major incidents might be handled via a separate *process* or by a *procedure*.

- Process: a set of activities designed to accomplish a specific objective.

- Procedure: documented steps for completing an activity.

So you might have a *procedure* for completing a single *process* step, such as escalation. As an example, one particular organisation with whom I worked used their normal Incident Management process for dealing with major incidents, but used a different escalation procedure as soon as an incident was categorised as *critical*.

Example Major Incident Escalation Procedure

- Escalate to Incident Manager
- Assemble major incident team
- Issue regular SMTP alerts/updates

These steps were designed to ensure that the management of such incidents was overseen by a senior member of staff, that senior management in the business always had visibility of progress and that major incidents were handled promptly and effectively.

The Incident Manager would immediately drop everything else and just focus on overseeing this one incident until it was resolved. The major incident team was immediately assembled from a group of nominated senior engineers and analysts who were on standby when not in the office. The Incident Manager would monitor and track progress and ensure that SMTP alerts were regularly issued to senior staff.

Whichever method is chosen, the goal is to recognise incidents that are critical, early in the incident lifecycle, and ensure they get the right level of priority and resource allocation, in a timely fashion, in order to deal with them efficiently and effectively.

In a similar fashion, it can often be very helpful to predefine steps for the handling of other types of non-critical incidents that occur regularly. Such a set of predefined steps is known as an *incident model*.

Incident Model: a set of predefined steps for dealing with a common type of incident.

ITIL® is very fond of the use of models. We don't just have incident models; we have request models, problem models, change models and so on. In all cases they are a set of predefined steps for dealing with a common issue, be it a service request, an incident, a problem or a change. One of the benefits of using models is that, once defined, they can be very easily automated.

As an example of the use of a model, think about what happens when someone fills-up their email inbox quota. They call the Service Desk, of course, and they are usually told that they need to archive some information and to work within their allocated quota for disk space. However, it is not uncommon for users to object to this and many organisations have a simple set of steps for dealing with this scenario.

- User to get approval from Line Manager
- Request passed to Capacity Management
- Capacity Management increase quota by 10%
- Finance (charging) notified of increased quota

In essence, the idea is that the user must first make their case for the quota increase to their own Line Manager and then, if approved, the request is processed by the Capacity Management process. This simple set of steps is an example of a *request model*.

Related Processes

A common approach to learning about the Service Management discipline involves considering each individual process in isolation. There is nothing wrong with that approach except that it may carry with it the implication that processes actually operate that way i.e. in isolation. But the truth is that they are actually operating simultaneously, not sequentially, and they are continually supporting each other.

In this book, we are primarily considering the Incident Management process. However, as you will have noted, we have mentioned a number of other Service Management processes in passing. The purpose of this section is to raise your awareness of how the Incident Management process interacts with other service Management processes.

When conducting an *initial diagnosis*, the Service Desk staff are making extensive use of the databases in the CMS (Configuration Management System) which are populated and maintained by other processes. In particular, note that the CMDB (Configuration Management Database) is maintained by the Service Asset & Configuration Management process and the KEDB (Known Error Database) is maintained by the Problem Management process.

After the analysis, when Incident Management requires something to be changed, you will recall that it initiates the change by raising an RFC (Request for Change) which not only ensures the change takes place, but also ensures that it is recorded in the CMDB (Configuration Management Database).

So, both the Change Management process and the Service Asset & Configuration Management process are involved.

When certain types of incident are reported, especially those relating to capacity, availability and security, they would typically be escalated to the relevant processes (Capacity Management, Availability Management and Information Security Management) which provide a point of focus for such incidents.

So, as you can hopefully now appreciate, Service Management processes actually work together to provide what the user experiences, in much the same way as the components of an engine work together to provide a car with its drive.

Closely Related Processes

The following Service Management processes are very closely related to the Incident Management process:

- Event Management
- Request Fulfilment
- Problem Management

Event Management is the process responsible for detecting events, making sense of them and then triggering the appropriate control action(s). As mentioned earlier, an event is in itself, not an incident. However, some events, for example, warning of imminent failure, have a level of significance that warrants that an incident record be raised and the situation be dealt with proactively. And certain events do indeed indicate that an incident has occurred.

For completeness, here an example of an Event Management process:

- Event Detection
- Event Filtering
- Significance Assigned
- Control Action Initiated

There are many items of hardware, software and firmware that are capable of producing event notifications; often, they are sent in SNMP (Simple Network Management Protocol). Much of this SNMP traffic does not indicate that anything unusual is happening; it is just part of the normal operation of the network. So, following the detection of event notifications, the process filters out events of this nature, effectively separating signal from noise, so that the significance of the remaining events can then be assessed in order to trigger the appropriate action.

Event Significance

- Informational: this type of event does not require any immediate corrective action. They are simply logged for future reference.

- Warning: this event type indicates that a device or service is approaching a threshold.

- Exception: means that a service or device is currently operating outside its normal parameters.

Note that a service or device that is operating abnormally (i.e. an exception) does not necessarily indicate that an incident has occurred, though this is certainly a strong possibility. Both exception events and warning events are analysed to determine what control action should be taken and the Event Management process actually initiates that action. The action might be to raise an incident record, a problem record, an RFC (Request for Change) or to start an automated script programmed with a prepared response – or even, some combination of those actions.

From the foregoing, we can see that Event Management is one way that incident records are raised automatically and it follows that the more we focus on detecting and dealing with events, the more proactive we will become in the prevention and management of incidents.

Request Fulfilment

Many calls to the Service Desk are not made for the purpose of reporting incidents, but are made for a variety of other reasons. Some examples are: to request information, to make a complaint, to request a password reset, to request access to software. All of these are examples of *service requests*.

No diagnosis or corrective action is required because no services are adversely affected. All that needs to happen is to log a service request and route it to the appropriate fulfilment team after any necessary approvals have been obtained.

Here an example of a Request Fulfilment process:

- Logging
- Approval
- Routing

- Fulfilment
- Closure

During the normal progress of the logging and categorising of incidents i.e. in the Incident Management process, some calls which effectively begin as incidents will be re-categorised as *service request* and then routed off to the Request Fulfilment process. This often happens because, the user may not be aware that the difficulty they are experiencing is not actually caused by an incident; for example, in the case of a password reset.

Service requests will often make use of a *request model* for their fulfilment and the necessary changes are usually *standard* i.e. changes that are pre-authorised by the Change Management process.

Types of Change

- Standard Change: pre-approved by Change Management

- Normal Change: goes to the CAB (Change Advisory Board) for consideration

- Emergency Change: goes to the ECAB (Emergency CAB) for consideration

The reason for having a separate Request Fulfilment process is to prevent the Incident Management and Change Management processes from becoming clogged up with low risk, frequently occurring requests by providing a way of dealing with them in an efficient and timely manner.

Before moving on, perhaps it is worth discussing whether or not, a password reset should be categorised as a service request. There are certainly organisations that do treat password resets as incidents and also many that don't. So which is correct? In practice, it is for your organisation to decide; in order words, it is a matter of individual policy.

However, you should note that the ITIL® guidance is in favour of treating password resets as *service requests* as they fit the criteria i.e. they are low risk and frequently occurring. You should also bear in mind that, if you were to treat them as incidents, your incident stats would become skewed and that would not be helpful to Service Level Management. Part of the Service Level Manager role, of course, involves reporting on service availability to customers and such reports make extensive use of incident data.

Problem Management

It is very important to gain a clear understanding of the relationship between incidents and problems.

The difference between an incident and a problem is that an incident is an interruption or degradation of a service, whereas a problem is an underlying cause. Incident Management is all about restoring normal service, whereas Problem Management is about figuring out why the incident happened in the first place and eradicating any underlying causes that might cause the incident to recur.

As an example, supposing a hard disk had failed in a server, resulting in a server crash. That is an incident and the Incident Management process would be used to deal with it. It would escalate the matter to the appropriate specialist who would typically raise an RFC (Request for Change) and get the hard disk replaced.

But suppose that a few months later, exactly the same thing happened again i.e. the new disk failed. Well, clearly we have another incident and again, the Incident Management process would log and investigate the matter.

However, repeating incidents are often an indication that a deeper level of investigation is required and that is why we have the Problem Management process i.e. to raise a separate problem record and mount an investigation into why the hard disk is repeatedly failing. It could be that there is another issue – perhaps a faulty power supply – which is periodically causing the disk to fail and that is the problem that needs to be addressed i.e. the underlying cause of the incidents. Problem Management, in this case, would also raise an RFC in order to get the faulty power supply changed.

Spotting recurring incidents and identifying incidents that might recur and then escalating them to Problem Management – to mount the deeper investigation into finding the underlying causes(s) – is one way that the Incident Management process supports the Problem Management process.

Problem Management, in turn, supports the Incident Management process by producing *workarounds* (temporary solutions) and documenting them in the KEDB (Known Error Database), one of the many databases in the CMS (Configuration Management System). This database is very useful, particularly to Service Desk staff when they are dealing with users as they report incidents, enabling them to reduce impact by providing these temporary solutions, at first point of contact, whilst a permanent solution is being worked out.

Note: If you would like to learn more about Problem Management, please see my book <u>Problem Management for Newbies</u> which is now available at all good online stores.

Integrated Toolset

When choosing the toolset to be used for Service Management, it is useful to bear in mind that there are two broad approaches that may be taken: you could use a *proprietary toolset* that effectively promises to provide a one-stop solution, or you could use a *best of breed* approach by mixing and matching various specialised tools to give you the functionality you require.

Either way, it is useful to bear in mind that you should design your processes first and then choose tools that allow you to work the way you want. Do not do the reverse i.e. choosing the tools first and then adjusting your working methods to fit in with the way they operate. This may sound like an obvious requirement, but you would be surprised at how often people get this the wrong way around. For example, bearing in mind the idea of *incident models* (which is a way you can automate activities such as escalation) you would probably want to select a toolset that allowed you to design and make use of them.

Similarly, the concept of the SKMS (Service Knowledge Management System) with its integrated CMS (Configuration Management System) containing the various databases we have discussed, is probably another major consideration you would wish to include in your statement of requirements for you toolset.

Do not assume that all Service Management toolsets will provide you with the functionality outlined in the ITIL® guidance, even if they have some approval logo stamped on the box. When V3 of ITIL® was first released, I remember attending a show and visiting six different vendor stands, none of whom were able to show me an SKMS that matched the ITIL® guidance. Of course, that was back in 2007 and things have significantly changed since then, but the lesson remains ... don't assume!

Conducting a MOSCOW brainstorming session is a very useful first step.

MOSCOW Analysis

M – What Must it Have
S – What Should it Have
C – What Could it Have
W – What Won't it Have

Get senior support analysts, especially any who hold the ITIL® Expert qualification, involved in your brainstorming session and use the MOSCOW format to arrive at your initial statement of requirements.

In Closing

Incident Management is one of the most visible processes within the whole Service Management discipline and the Service Desk function itself might be described as the face of IT to the organisation. Much of how IT is perceived within your organisation is therefore heavily influenced by these two factors i.e. how users are dealt with by the Service Desk and how efficiently and effectively the Incident Management process operates.

Effectiveness: achieving the desired goal(s)
Efficiency: operating in the optimal way

Gauging the effectiveness of your Service Desk and Incident Management process can be done by developing performance metrics and also by surveying the customers. Surveying customers is often done immediately following incident closure, when the details of the interaction are fresh in the mind. But a regular, perhaps annual, customer satisfaction survey can also be a very useful tool for identifying improvement opportunities.

Example Service Desk Metrics

- Percentage of Incidents Resolved at Desk
- Average Time to Resolve at Desk
- Average Time to Escalate when not Resolved
- Average Time to Close when Resolved

Example Incident Management Metrics

- Average Time to Resolve Incident
- Percentage of Incidents Reopened
- Percentage of Incidents Incorrectly Categorised
- Percentage of Incidents Incorrectly Routed

The above are just suggestions, of course. They are all good, practical suggestions, but you should really think about how to measure the performance of your own Service Desk and Incident Management process as part of its design and ongoing improvement. Don't be tempted to measure and report against too many metrics. Initially, just decide upon a few meaningful metrics and work with them for a while.

Introduce new measurements only when there is a specific need that is not met by your existing measurement framework and never produce reports just for the sake of doing it. Every time you do produce a report, ask the question, *who is it for and is it still necessary?*

In addition to measuring performance, further metrics might be established for other purposes. For example, to calculate the staffing levels required by the Service Desk, a metric relating to the volume of calls per day, week and month can be very useful. Whilst it is impractical to provide recommendations about how to correlate exact numbers of staff with incident volume, it is possible to arrive at a good approximation of what is likely to be needed by considering the anticipated call volume and the number of existing analysts that handle the current demand.

Continuous Improvement

When we introduce any process into an organisation, it is not mature i.e. the process itself needs to be improved until it is operating in an optimal way and this is true for any process, of course, not just Incident Management. So it is well worth reflecting upon how mature your Incident Management process currently is and decide upon what steps you can take to improve its maturity.

In the ITIL® guidance, there is a process maturity framework (PMF) that can be used to assess the maturity of your processes. Here is a brief description of the five levels of maturity defined:

PMF Levels

Level 1: Processes are described as 'Ad hoc' i.e. although they work, they are not documented and not formalised. They work because of the commitment and flexibility of the individuals involved to ensure the right thing is always done.

Level 2: Processes are described as 'Repeatable' i.e. they are documented but are often reactive and they are not measured and, hence, are difficult to improve.

Level 3 - Processes are described as 'Defined' i.e. they are well documented, they are measured and have reporting in place.

Level 4 - Processes are described as 'Managed' i.e. they are well-defined with both *manager* (concerned with monitoring & reporting) and *owner* (overall process accountability) roles operating and they are continuously improved.

Level 5 - Processes are described as 'Optimising' i.e. they have all the characteristics of a Level 4 process but additionally, they are truly business focused.

If you follow the recommendations of the ITIL® guidance, you should be able to continually improve your processes until they eventually reach Level 5 maturity.

If you consider the recommendation of integrating an Event Management process with your Incident Management process, for example, you can see how your Incident Management process can become much more proactive.

By assigning both owners and managers to your processes, you ensure they are effectively monitored, reported upon and continuously improved. Note that the responsibilities of these two roles can be combined into a single role.

Utilising an SKMS (Service Knowledge Management System) with its various integrated management information systems (xMIS) will enable you to properly define and document every aspect of your service management processes. It is also the place where data collected by the various Service Management processes gets crunched into valuable knowledge upon which process owners, who have overall accountability for each process, can act in order to improve their individual processes.

Finally, be aware that there are very many recommendations throughout the ITIL® guidance that pertain to encouraging IT service operations to adopt more of a business focussed approach. Within the Incident Management process, the discussion around prioritisation, as you will be aware, is very much concerned with ensuring the needs of the business are put first.

If you wish to improve your Service Management capability within Incident Management or, for that matter, any other area, remember that Rome was not built in a day. Adopt a philosophy of continuous improvement. Get your process *owner* and *manager* roles in place and begin monitoring, measuring, reporting and analysing your data to identify improvement opportunities. Select the best ideas, implement them and measure again to see if your action was successful in delivering the expected improvement.

Then ... when you are ready, do it again ... and again.

Allow for periods of consolidation in between improvement initiatives, so that people get used to new ways of operating. But stay focussed on your goal i.e. to improve your processes all the way to Level 5. If you keep that focus and you continually improve, you can be assured that will eventually get there!

Part 3

Problem Management for Newbies

Foreword to Problem Management

Problem Management is about preventing problems and resulting incidents from occurring, eliminating recurring incidents and minimising the impact of incidents that cannot be prevented. It is a process that delivers significant value to businesses by reducing the downtime and disruption caused by service interruptions.

Getting better at Problem Management means that far less effort is spent in 'fire-fighting' and dealing with repeating incidents as root-causes are systematically identified and eliminated. In addition to reducing the number and duration of service outages, an effective process will significantly improve Service Desk resolution times and increase customer satisfaction levels yet, according to Gartner (2011), only 20% of organisations have well-integrated Incident and Problem Management processes in place.

Whilst many books have been written on the subject of generic problem-solving and logical or critical thinking, there are comparatively few that consider these skills within the context of Problem Management and the ITIL® Best Practice framework from the OGC (Office of Government Commerce), hence the need for this book which provides a comprehensive introduction to this important discipline.

Introduction to Problem Management

Problem-solving has always interested me, long before I ever learned anything about ITIL®. The ability to set yourself a huge goal, way outside of your comfort zone; to say, effectively, 'I am going to achieve that' when you have absolutely no idea how you will do it, and then to work your way forward, solving all of the problems and overcoming all of the obstacles that stand in your way is, I believe, one of the most important life-skills you could ever master.

My early fascination with the subject led me to read many of the books of the world-renowned expert Edward De Bono, the originator of the phrase 'lateral thinking'. His work in this area is seminal. I remember on one occasion, bringing one of his books home from the local library in my home town. It was his *Five Day Course in Thinking*. The basic idea was to work through the book at the rate of one problem per day. But my dad thought that was simply a waste of time and, because I just couldn't hold him back, together, we worked right through all of the problems in a few hours. I learned a lot by solving those problems, including to not show my dad any of the books I brought home from the library, from that moment forward.

Another thing I learned, as a result of working through the course, was that my ability to solve problems did seem to have sharpened a little. At the time, I had no explanation for that effect. In fact, I was not at all sure that it was not simply my imagination. After all, why should learning how to solve problems that involved knives and bottles have any effect on my ability to solve problems that were more relevant and important to me? Since then, I have come to understand that learning how to solve problems causes our brains to become 'rewired' so that the kind of thinking necessary for problem-solving comes to us much more naturally; we see things differently, we begin to make deductions more quickly and we do indeed get better.

By the way, any kind of learning involves growing connections in our brain. They are known as axons and dendrites, and learning new concepts actually involves growing them or strengthening the connections we already have in place. This is one of the reasons that learning is difficult; it is why learning anything at all takes time and repetition. But once those new pathways in our brain become established and well-used, we then have the ability to use them at our instant disposal. Our neural network of connections between brain cells is unique to ourselves. It is the root-cause of what makes us good at those things we can do very easily and without much conscious thought.

So, as we work our way through this book, we will look at the ITIL® process for managing problems and we will consider the kinds of techniques that are useful for problem-solving within an IT context. But we will also look at other problems that are designed to help you sharpen your ability to think. We will consider why it is that some problems seem impossible to solve and yet, when they are eventually solved, we wonder why we could not see the solution in the first place. Take your time with the material. Bear in mind that you are, metaphorically, rewiring your brain as you work through these problems and you are developing or sharpening a skill that will serve you in any occupation and in all walks of life.

ITIL® & Problem Management

The ITIL® framework of Best Practice for IT Service Management from the OGC (Office of Government Commerce) consists of a set of five volumes which together make up what has become known as the *core guidance*.

Here is a list of the Official ITIL® publications in the core guidance:

- Service Strategy (SS)
- Service Design (SD)
- Service Transition (ST)
- Service Operation (SO)
- Continual Service Improvement (CSI)

Just from the titles, you can see that the structure of the guidance follows the *lifecycle* of a service all the way from concept, through design, build, test and into the live environment where it gets continually improved until it is eventually retired.

At a top level, here's what each of those volumes are about:

Service Strategy

This book is about the future and, in particular, it is about the future of the portfolio of services offered by the service provider. The guidance concerns top level business thinking around strategic direction and effectively managing the portfolio so as to achieve the business strategy, expressed in terms of plans, policies, and vision.

Here are the processes described in Service Strategy:

- Strategy Management for IT Services
- Financial Management for IT Services
- Service Portfolio Management
- Demand Management
- Business Relationship Management

Service Design

The guidance in this book concerns the design of services, naturally, but it is also concerned with the design of other aspects of service management such as processes, metrics, architectures and tools. Service Design translates the requirements of the organisation into a package of plans and specifications and then hands them over to the next phase of the lifecycle.

Here are the processes included in Service Design:

- Design Coordination
- Capacity Management
- IT Service Continuity Management (ITSCM)
- Availability Management
- Service Catalogue Management
- Information Security management
- Service Level Management
- Supplier Management

Service Transition

This book deals with checking and executing the plans prepared by the previous phase (Service Design) so that a new (or significantly changed) service is gracefully introduced (built, tested and deployed) into the live environment when it is handed over to the next phase of the lifecycle for ongoing support. The central theme of this book concerns the protection of the live environment i.e. ensuring that the introduction of significant changes do not adversely affect the organisation.

Here are the processes in Service Transition:

- Transition Planning
- Release & Deployment Management
- Change Evaluation
- Service Validation & Testing
- Service Asset & Configuration Management
- Change Management
- Knowledge Management

Service Operation

This book is about the ongoing support of services that are already deployed within the live environment. The guidance concerns both the handling of service interruptions and also dealing with various other types of request made by users. In addition, there is guidance on proactive activities designed to reduce service outages and eliminate their causes.

Here are the processes discussed in Service Operation:

- Problem Management
- Incident management

- Request Fulfilment
- Event Management
- Access Management

Continual Service Improvement

The Continual Service Improvement (CSI) volume concerns the improvement not only of services but of every aspect of service management including processes, entire lifecycle phases and service management as a whole. Embracing the thinking of William Edwards Deming, the guidance deals with the delivery of measureable, incremental improvements that move the service provider in the direction of the strategic vision.

Here is the single process included in CSI:

- 7-Step Improvement Process

From the foregoing, we can see that Problem Management is a process defined within the Service Operation volume of the ITIL® core guidance. More specifically, Problem Management is the process that is responsible for identifying and eliminating the underlying causes of service interruptions.

This book provides a comprehensive introduction to the Problem Management discipline. For readers who require a comprehensive introduction to ITIL® and IT Service Management as a whole, please see my book IT Service Management for Newbies which is now available in all good online stores.

What is a Problem?

A good place to start is by looking at what we mean when we say we have a problem. In our normal English usage of the word, when we say that we have a problem, we mean that there is something that needs to be solved. If we are at point A and we want to go to point B but we don't know the way, then we have a problem. On the other hand, if we *do* know the way, then we have a task to be performed, but not a problem to be solved.

If we now turn to the ITIL® definition of a problem, we find it is 'the cause of one or more incidents' and an incident is an 'interruption or degradation' of a service. It is the difference between cause and effect: the incident is the effect and the problem is the underlying cause. Just to make sure we get the right idea, let's consider some examples.

Supposing one day, as you entered your office, you flicked the light switch and the light bulb blew – that would effectively be an incident. You would, of course, get the maintenance man to replace the bulb and that is a good analogy for what Incident Management does i.e. it 'restores normal service as soon as possible'. But, suppose that the next day, the same thing happened i.e. you entered your office, flicked the switch ... and the same light bulb went bang. It is still an incident – a recurring incident certainly – but still an incident. The maintenance man scratches his head, changes the bulb and tests the switch – again, this is effectively Incident Management – and everything seems to be fine. Now, what if, the very next day, exactly the same thing happens again?

In that situation, you still have an incident to be dealt with, but if your maintenance man only ever does Incident Management, all he will ever do is change the bulb! And, he could get very good at changing bulbs too. He might even leave you a few spares as you seem to be getting through them rather quickly. The recurring incident is not, in itself, a problem, but it is an indication that a problem exists and the process of working out why the bulb is repeatedly being blown and dealing with the underlying cause is effectively what the Problem Management process does. Perhaps, staying with our illustration, there is a wire that is loosely connected. When the maintenance man eventually finds that loose wire and tightens the connection, removing the cause of the repeat incidents, then he is doing Problem Management.

Here's an IT example ...

Let's imagine that, one day, our email service stops running for some reason. If that were to happen, the Service Desk would, of course, soon hear about it from our users. This is an incident, of course, and we would kick off the Incident Management process by logging the call.

For completeness, here is the ITIL® Incident Management process ...

- Logging
- Categorisation
- Prioritisation
- Analysis
- Functional Escalation
- Monitoring
- Tracking

- Closing

Logging – involves recording the incident in a database

Categorisation – hardware or software; which application etc

Prioritisation – involves setting an initial priority

Analysis – is an initial attempt at resolution

Functional Escalation – getting the call to the right specialist

Monitoring/Tracking – keeping an eye on incident progress

Closing – requires confirmation from the user

Let's say that the call is escalated to our expert on the email service and, as part of his investigation, he reboots the email server. Once the server is up and running again, the email service starts as usual and everything seems to be operating normally. Bearing in mind that the goal of Incident Management is 'restoration of normal service as soon as possible' the incident is actually resolved.

But a few months later, suppose the email service stops running again. It is a bit like the loose wire isn't it? There is a recurring incident and that is suggesting that there is likely to be a common underlying cause that needs to be investigated and this is what Problem Management would do. The incident would be dealt with by the Incident Management process but, in alignment with the organisation's policy concerning repeat incidents, the matter might also be escalated to the Problem Manager to raise a separate problem record and begin the investigation to look for the underlying cause – perhaps it might be that the server operating system needs a patch.

To remove the underlying cause, something generally needs to be changed; in the above example, a software update is required. So the Problem Management process would actually raise the necessary RFC (Request for Change) which would then go to the Change Management process to be progressed. We'll be looking at the Problem Management process in some detail later. But, for now, I just want you to understand what a problem is, both in the normal English language usage of the word and also from an ITIL® perspective.

To recap:

- Normal usage: a problem is something that needs to be solved

- ITIL®: a problem is the underlying cause of one or more incidents

As you can quite easily see from the above examples, there is no contradiction between those two definitions. The business of finding and eradicating underlying causes of incidents necessarily involves defining and solving problems. That said, there is a very clear distinction between the terms *problem* and *incident* as they are used in ITIL ®. They are certainly related, but they are not the same thing. Incidents never become problems, even when they recur. The recurring incident is *not* a problem, but it *is* an indication that a problem exists.

By the way, recurring incidents are not the only way to identify the existence of problems as we shall see. However, spotting recurring incidents and escalating them to the Problem Management process, not for incident resolution but to eradicate underlying causes, is an important way that the Incident Management process works with Problem Management.

Proactive & Reactive Elements

The examples we have discussed so far are reactive i.e. something happened and we dealt with it (Incident Management) and if the same thing recurred sufficiently often, we looked into the cause and dealt with it too (Problem Management) – and that's Reactive Problem Management because the process was triggered by the repeat incident.

These days, it is not uncommon to hear of car manufacturers recalling a particular model to have some amendment made to the steering or the brakes and this is a very good example of Proactive Problem Management at work. In this situation, we have not had an incident but we are, nevertheless, taking proactive action to prevent possible future incidents.

Way back, in the nineteen seventies, there was a series of DC-10 plane crashes.

When the first DC-10 was being tested at the firm's factory in Long Beach, California, in May 1970, an incident occurred that would come back and haunt the airliner in the coming decade. During cabin pressurisation tests, one of the jet's cargo doors blew open and a large section of the cabin floor collapsed. The problem was dismissed at the time as a result of "human failure" and the airliner went on to enter service with American Airlines just over a year later.

Yet in 1972, an American Airlines DC-10 suffered a sudden loss of cabin pressure at 12,000ft and part of the cabin floor collapsed into the cargo hold. Once the aircraft was safely on the ground it was found one of the cargo doors had opened in flight, causing the depressurisation. The incident was blamed by Douglas on the door having been forced shut by a ramp service agent on the ground using his knee.

The US National Transportation Safety Board (NTSB) made two urgent recommendations for changes to the DC-10's cargo doors and Douglas assured the authorities that the changes could be made during regular maintenance checks. But the crash of a Turkish Airlines' DC-10, 10 minutes after take-off from Paris in March 1974 put the cargo door problems in a whole new light. All 346 people on board the flight died.

-   BBC News UK http://www.bbc.co.uk/news/uk-21059525

The DC-10 problem was the design of the cargo hatch door. It opened outward, rather than inward, to allow for more space in the hold. But the locking mechanism was faulty and sometimes the door dislodged. This caused catastrophic decompression and the collapse of the cabin floor. Underneath the cabin floor were the cables used to control the plane and if they were sheared the aircraft was doomed.

The American Airlines plane (Flight 96) was a complete write-off, and was successfully landed only because the cabin floor on that particular plane had been reinforced. The important steering cables were therefore not severed and they were thus able to retain sufficient control of the aircraft. The reason the cabin floor had been reinforced was that they happened to be transporting a piano at the time. Unfortunately, the Turkish Airlines plane had no such modification and consequently, the cabin floor collapse turned out to be disastrous. These catastrophes are notable and infamous examples of the failure of Problem Management.

In principle, it should have been possible to have prevented both of these aviation accidents with proper Proactive Problem Management as the "human error" they identified during testing was in fact subsequently repeated on the ground by a "service agent". These tragic incidents also illustrate that it is perfectly possible for problems to exist in the infrastructure that have not yet caused incidents. The fact that they were flying DC-10s for about a year before the American Airlines incident serves as a stark reminder as to why the discipline of Proactive Problem Management is so vitally important, especially when human life is potentially on the line.

Here's another scenario for you to think about:

Supposing we were supporting an important service that had suffered from repeated outages over a period of about nine months. Let's say that, on each occasion, the server had been experiencing hard disk errors and that each time, an engineer had changed the disk to resolve the incident. But now, the matter has been escalated to Problem management for further investigation.

After discussions with the vendor, the Problem Manager learned that if the serial number of the server was in a particular range, the power supply in the server would also need to be changed. The manufacturer had identified a problem batch of servers with under-rated power supplies and this was, in fact, the problem i.e. the reason that hard disks were malfunctioning. Given this scenario, after the Problem

Manager had addressed the matter of getting the power supply changed, what do you think he should do next?

I'll let you know what I think in a little while but get your Problem Manager hat on, think about the above question for a few minutes and try to come up with your own answer before you read on.

We can learn about the existence of problems in many different ways including simply being told by a manufacturer or a software vendor (as in the above example) that some problem exists. We may or may not have experienced any consequences i.e. it could be that no related incidents have been reported so far. But we can now act to assess the situation and take proactive action to eradicate underlying causes before they lead to incidents.

We will return to the subject of how you can identify the existence of problems, but for now, I just want you to be clear about the difference between *Proactive* and *Reactive* Problem Management.

   - Proactive: Fixing things before they cause incidents to happen

   - Reactive: Using the incident data to find and address underlying causes

Now – did you think about that question? Well, if your answer was that you would interrogate the CMDB (Configuration Management Database) to determine whether or not you have any additional servers supplied by that vendor and deployed in the live environment; servers which have never failed, and yet have their serial numbers in the faulty range – if you were thinking like that, then you my friend, are going to make an excellent Problem Manager. That is a good example of proactive thinking.

How Do We Identify Problems?

So far we have encountered two ways of identifying the existence of a problem: 1) a sequence of repeat incidents and 2) information provided directly by a supplier. A third possible way is when we receive multiple simultaneous incidents.

Consider the following situation:

The message came in the form of a sharp bang and vibration. Jack Swigert saw a warning light that accompanied the bang, and said, "Houston, we've had a problem here." I came on and told the ground that it was a main B bus undervolt. The time was 2108 hours on April 13.

Next, the warning lights told us we had lost two of our three fuel cells, which were our prime source of electricity. Our first thoughts were ones of disappointment, since mission rules forbade a lunar landing with only one fuel cell.

With warning lights blinking on, I checked our situation; the quantity and pressure gages for the two oxygen tanks gave me cause for concern. One tank appeared to be completely empty, and there were indications that the oxygen in the second tank was rapidly being depleted.

> - *Jim Lovell, Captain Apollo 13*
> *http://history.nasa.gov/SP-350/ch-13-1.html*

The story of Apollo 13, the third attempt at landing on the moon, is truly inspirational. As you can see from the above extract from Jim Lovell's account of the mission, it was actually

Jack Swigert, the command module pilot who originally said, "Huston, we've had a problem." Jim repeated the phrase after Huston asked for clarification.

Now that we understand the difference between incidents and problems, should Jack have said, "Huston, we have an incident?"

The answer is no! Jack was perfectly correct. Multiple incidents were, in fact, reported to Huston during those few minutes as you can clearly see from Jim's account. But Jack was right, those multiple simultaneous incidents were an indication that there was a common cause – something had caused an explosion.

Here are the incidents that were reported by the Apollo 13 crew:

- There was a sharp bang and vibration
- There is a main B bus undervolt
- We have lost two of our three fuel cells
- One [oxygen] tank appears to be completely empty
- The second [oxygen] tank is rapidly being depleted

The problem was that there was an under-rated component in the in the oxygen tank's circuitry; a thermostatic switch. When a higher voltage than the switch was designed to handle was passed through it, it welded the contacts shut and the switch could no longer function as intended. This caused the temperature in the oxygen tanks to rise unchecked, following the 'stirring' of the tanks. Eventually, the oxygen ignited. So you see, that one problem – an under-rated component – caused the explosion which led to multiple simultaneous incidents, which were the effects that the crew reported to Huston.

Another method of identifying the existence of problems, and one that is commonly used by the Problem Management process, is to utilise incident data to identify trends.

Here is a simple example of Trend Analysis:

Supposing that our incident stats show that, generally, we get somewhere around 30-50 calls per day to the Service Desk. However, every Monday, we regularly get about twice the average number of incidents. Now, of course, that shouldn't happen should it? If you think about what we, as a service provider, are doing: we are providing the same level of service every day, utilising exactly the same component parts and operating in the same way. So such a trend in the incident data – a big spike every Monday - would not be expected.

Of course, if you were looking at a very short time period, there might be valid reasons for such an observed effect. However, the longer the period that you are sampling, the less likely the above trend would be. But the trend is definitely there and so ... it *is* telling us something! In this situation, the Problem Manager would (after raising a problem record naturally) assemble a problem-solving group of specialists in order to brainstorm possible causes.

Effect: Big Spike of Incidents Every Monday

Possible Causes:

- Changes implemented over the weekend causing large number of knock-on incidents

- People forgetting their passwords

- People saving up incidents that occur over the weekend and waiting until Monday to report them

Perhaps you can think of some other possible causes.

Once we produce a list of possible causes, we can then take matters a step further and, by the process of elimination, arrive at the true cause. Once we understand the true cause, we can then take remedial action; we can raise an RFC (Request for Change) to get something changed if that is appropriate.

Supposing we have verified that the true cause happens to be badly managed changes that are being introduced over the weekend during our agreed *change window* (a period agreed with the business for making changes). What might we ask for in our RFC? In that situation, we might ask for our testing processes and procedures to be reviewed and improved. What if the cause was people forgetting their passwords? We might ask for our password policy to be reviewed and changed if necessary. What about people saving up their incidents until Monday morning? Perhaps that is acceptable; perhaps we might ask for Service Desk cover to be made available over the weekends.

The above is just a simple example of Trend Analysis to give you the basic idea. In summary, a very powerful technique used by Problem Management, Trend Analysis is the business of examining incident data, looking for patterns that should not exist, identifying trends in the data and asking the question: what is that trend telling us?

Here are the four methods we have discussed that can assist us in the identification of the existence of problems:

- Repeating incidents

- Information from another party (supplier, vendor, technician, partner etc)

- Multiple simultaneous incidents

- Trend Analysis using incident data

Problem Management could ask for just about anything to be changed if it is found to be the underlying cause of an incident or incidents. That does not mean to say that the change will actually take place, but it does mean that the proposal will be formally assessed by the Change Management process and approved and implemented if the relevant Change Authority (often the CAB – Change Advisory Board) is convinced of the need.

Creative Problem Solving

In order to examine how we normally tend to solve problems, reasoning forward from our understanding of the problem to eventually finding a solution, let's take a look at Edward De Bono's problem solving model. It is a useful model that neatly illustrates the five stages of our thinking.

Edward De Bono's Problem-Solving Model:

- Definition
- Logical Analysis
- Possible Solutions
- Decision
- Implementation

Just understanding that those five steps are involved is a very useful insight in itself. Without this understanding, your thinking is likely to be less structured, skipping about the various areas. But with this understanding, you have a basic roadmap for the thinking process. You can consciously move through the model step by step to arrive at your solution and then get on with implementing it.

Let's take a look at each step ...

Definition

Some problems really *are* problems of definition i.e. they will yield when we have them properly defined. Essentially, if your problem is defined as 'the lifts are too slow' then it is likely you will produce solutions involving faster motors and different gearing. On the other hand, if your problem is defined as 'people keep saying the lifts are too slow' you will definitely produce different types of solutions, such as muzak, mirrors, progress indicators etc.

How the definition of a problem affects the solutions we produce is an important point because – staying with our example - there is only so fast you can make a lift without also making the ride very uncomfortable. So, if making the lift go faster is not a realistic option and people *still* think the lifts are too slow, then you need to gain access to a different category of solution. This should convince you that getting the problem properly defined is an important first step.

Logical Analysis

It is often possible to make useful deductions from what we know or are given and sometimes, once we make a particular deduction, a solution will immediately become apparent. There are two types of deduction we can make. We can use logical reasoning to arrive at general conclusions - this is known as inductive reasoning - and we can also do the opposite i.e. we can arrive at specific conclusions, reasoning from general observations – this is deductive reasoning.

For example, if the cycle goes over a bump and the engine misfires, and then goes over another bump and the engine misfires, and then goes over another bump and the engine misfires, and then goes over a long smooth stretch of road and there is no misfiring, and then goes over a fourth bump and the engine misfires again, one can logically conclude that the misfiring is caused by the bumps. That is induction: reasoning from particular experiences to general truths.

Deductive inferences do the reverse. They start with general knowledge and predict a specific observation. For example, if, from reading the hierarchy of facts about the machine, the mechanic knows the horn of the cycle is powered exclusively by electricity from the battery, then he can logically infer that if the battery is dead the horn will not work. That is deduction.

- *Robert Pirsig*
Zen and the Art of Motorcycle Maintenance

The use of logical analysis is such a powerful tool that, when correctly applied, enables us, not only to know the answer, but to know that we know!

Possible Solutions

Generally, this step involves brainstorming. Once you have the problem defined and you have derived what you can from a logical perspective, you have done the spadework and now it is time to think about what can be done to address the issue. One thing I particularly like about De Bono's model is that it encourages the practitioner to brainstorm an array of possible solutions and not simply to go with the first idea that comes up. This is very powerful because accessing the best solution often does require us to stretch our minds and consider unusual thoughts and ideas.

Working in problem-solving groups, the facilitator should simply note ideas as they are suggested and then keep the group working on the production of further possibilities. The key thing is to *not* judge ideas as they are proposed. There are a couple of reasons for this. Firstly, creativity and humour are very closely related and often things that are said in jest turn out to contain the seed of a very good idea. Secondly, if you do judge a person's idea by immediately telling them why it will not work, you will not only risk losing that person's creative input, you will also close off the possible modifications of the idea that other people would have proposed. Always bear in mind that the best solutions are sometimes to be found in apparently ridiculous suggestions.

Decision Making

With an array of solutions available, it is often an easy matter to select the best. In a group situation, you might simply take a show of hands. If you think that a particularly powerful personality might sway the decisions of other people present, you can get everybody to write their suggestions on yellow *post-it* notes and then stick them on a board, collating the ideas as you go. The consensus view will then become immediately obvious.

Sometimes, it can be helpful to ask people to say what they 'feel' rather than what they 'think' i.e. to encourage them to express their gut instincts. The reason is that sometimes, for a variety of reasons, people cannot express, logically, why they think a particular course of action is correct but despite this, their subconscious mind (psychologists tell us that most of our thinking is subconscious) may have given them the right, or best, answer. So allowing people to express their feelings without having to justify them is sometimes a very profitable exercise.

Finally, as a leader (if you are) sometimes the final decision just has to be yours. Not because of ego or accountability, but because that's why you were selected for the role, to exercise leadership. Good leaders use the above tools, they find out what the team thinks, they utilise logical and intuitive methods and then they make, and stand, by their decisions.

Implementation

This step is where you create and execute an action plan for resolving the problem. In certain situations, the plan might consist, simply, of a list of activities and the allocation of roles and responsibilities; in other situations, much more detailed planning will be required. The plan should be as detailed as you need it to be, but no more.

At this stage the problem has been apparently solved and you are getting into the implementation of the solution, whatever that happens to be. However, it is still possible that during implementation, you may encounter some situation you had not anticipated. Your original solution is probably perfectly good, but you now realise that there is a bit of adjustment necessary.

If you get stuck during the implementation phase, then you can think of it as simply having another problem to solve and you can do that by going through the steps again with a new problem definition i.e. just see the situation as a roadblock. Define the new problem in terms of 'how do we get around this roadblock' and work your way through the steps again.

Problem Types

Each of the above steps is very important and you can get stuck at any stage. It is sometimes difficult to get the problem properly defined but until you do, the best solution will likely remain inaccessible.

Here is a famous problem - see if you can solve it:

You are in a darkened room, without windows, which has no fixtures or furniture of any kind. You know that somewhere within in the room there is a diamond and your task is to locate it. What will your strategy be for finding the gem?

-   Kaplan

Think about this problem for a few minutes to see if you can solve it before moving on. There is more than one possible answer but the best answer will occur to you when you have the problem properly defined in your mind.

There was one time when I had been playing football with my son and a group of kids at the local park. At the end of the game on my way back to the car, I realised that I had lost my keys. Clearly they had fallen from my pocket during the game. Returning to the pitch, I realised the grass was long enough to effectively conceal them and I would need to be right on top of them to see them. It was not a dissimilar problem and I needed to find those keys.

What I eventually did was walk up and down the length of the field in columns, scanning a width of about three of four feet with each pass. I eventually found them after about 10 minutes using this approach. Of course, your answer to the diamond problem could be something similar but you will come up with a much better solution once you **define** the problem in your mind as 'find the light switch' rather than 'find the gem'.

Now let's look at a second type of problem and, to get us started, let's use a classic example. In 17th century England, it was assumed that, unlike sheep (for which you could regularly observe black variants) swans were always white. If that *premise* were true, then you can logically deduce the colour of any bird you can correctly identify as a swan. For example, if at twilight, you happened to see the profile of a bird that you were pretty sure was a swan, then with equal surety, you would know that it was white.

- All swans are white ... premise

- That bird is a swan ... observation

- Therefore, that bird is white ... logical deduction

After James Cook had 'discovered' Australia, and European explorers actually observed black swans for the first time, the *all-swans-are white* premise was, in fact, show to be false and that, of course, means that our conclusion is false too, despite the logic being impeccable.

But logic is a very powerful tool that can enable us to know the answer to very many problems, provided our reasoning is sound and our premises are correct. Again, here is a classic problem and, I would really like you to think hard about it before reading on and finding the solution.

Which of the following statements (A, B, C or D) is true?

A. The number of false statements here is one.

B. The number of false statements here is two.

C. The number of false statements here is three.

D. The number of false statements here is four.

The above logic problem is one that I always use at my workshops and it is a very interesting problem indeed. It can often get people disagreeing and even arguing about their answers but there really is only one correct answer and, if your logic is good, you will not only find the right answer, you will know you have found it too.

Very often, at my workshops, people will answer that either none of the statements are true or that they are all true. But both of those answers are *intuitive*, not logical. Intuition does indeed have its uses in problem-solving, as we discussed above, but it has no place in logic and, if you really worked on the above problem long enough, you would eventually conclude that *statement C* is indeed true.

The power of logic is that you can make correct deductions reasoning from trustworthy information. In other words, when you are faced with some problem to solve, you can find out more than you are given, or told, by correctly **analysing** the facts.

The third type of problem is characterised by a lack of inspiration. This is where you have the problem properly defined and you have also applied logic to deduce what you can. In other words, you have a complete understanding of the problem. But nevertheless, you still cannot think of any possible solutions. Earlier, I mentioned the work of Edward De Bono, much of which has been about the subject of *lateral thinking*. This *lack-of-inspiration* type of problem is where lateral thinking is most useful.

In a nutshell, lateral thinking is a technique that turns the reasoning process around so that you access the answer first and then you figure out why it is the right answer. It may sound odd to you, it may sound illogical or it may even sound silly. But lateral thinking is a technique you can profitably turn to when you are faced with seemingly insurmountable problems.

Here is an example of the type of problem that gives lateral thinking a bad name:

In the middle of the ocean is a yacht. Several corpses are floating in the water nearby. Can you work out what happened?

With a bit of thought, I am sure you could come up with many possible solutions.

For example, perhaps the people went for a swim and were attacked by sharks. The sharks didn't eat them but injured them badly enough so that they were unable to swim back to the boat and so they eventually drowned. Or perhaps, those people were robbed, killed and thrown overboard by pirates. Or perhaps, there had been a storm and they were thrown overboard and drowned. Perhaps, it was the result of a lover's pact to end their lives by suicide — even if there were three of them (I can think of various reasons why). Perhaps that is just what happens when you sail through the Bermuda Triangle.

These types of problem are not entirely without value because they can be used to help stimulate your creative ability for generating *possibilities*. In that respect they do have a limited amount of practical use. But, in my opinion, many of the supposed lateral thinking problems we often find are pretty useless in terms of developing our ability to think laterally and they are also useless in terms of serving as an illustration of the technique.

Lateral thinking is coming at a problem from a different angle and often, just understanding that this needs to be done is enough to give your thinking a little push in the right direction. I don't think it is true, but the following story is a good illustration of lateral thinking.

There was a man serving a prison sentence who was well aware that his mail was being routinely screened. In a letter from his wife, she mentioned that she wanted to begin planting the garden, but that the ground was so hard it was going to be very difficult to turn.

In his reply the man wrote, "Good grief! Don't dig up the garden, that's where I hid the money!" Soon, the prisoner received another letter from his wife saying that the police had descended on the house and dug up the garden.

To illustrate how lateral thinking can be useful for solving problems, consider the following challenging problem from Edward De Bono's *Five Day Course in Thinking* …

Take 4 bottles and 4 knives. Place the bottles in a square configuration on a table, so they are just further apart than the length of a knife. Using the knives create a platform between the bottles that will support a glass of water. None of the knives may touch the desk.

This is a problem I often use in my workshops and sometimes people solve it within the time I usually allow, which is just 15 minutes. However, most people cannot solve it in that time. Edward De Bono suggests allowing yourself a whole day to try to solve it. There is a clue that appears below but try your best to solve it before reading on.

It is a brilliant problem. One of the things it illustrates so beautifully is that just because we can't see a solution – no matter how hard we try - does not mean to say that a simple, elegant solution does not actually exist. People usually think they already understand that important truth but in reality, it is often only head knowledge. In other words, when faced with real problems in life, they often fail to demonstrate this crucial fact and consequently give up far too soon.

One way of using lateral thinking is to take solutions (to other problems) that already exist and then see if we can apply them to our problem. It does not matter one bit if the solutions we are considering are related to the problem we are trying to solve. If you solved the above problem, then well done; if you haven't yet, then here is an unrelated solution I would like you to think about ...

Imagine that you have just filled a cardboard box with items and you now want to seal it in some way. But you do not have any tape or other items that might help. So you decide to fold the lid in a particular way. This, of course, is an unrelated solution with which you will already be familiar. Now, see if you can apply that solution to the knives-and-bottles problem above.

The chances are that you will be able to adapt the cardboard box solution to provide you with the solution to the Edward De Bono problem – and when you do that, you are using lateral thinking!

When we are completely stuck, we need to gain access to a different type of thinking and that is what lateral thinking – sometimes called *thinking-outside-the-box* - is all about. For problems that seem insurmountable, when our normal ability to think of **possibilities** seems to have deserted us, then lateral thinking can help to provide access to a solution.

Without the ability to give our thinking this kind of mental nudge, out of its familiar territory, it remains constrained. As Abraham Maslow, so eloquently put it, "when you only have a hammer, there is a tendency to see every problem as a nail."

When we finally have the solution, that we were initially unable to see, it is easy to see why the solution fits the problem. But it is because the solution required some kind of mental shift away from our normal forward reasoning process that the solution was very difficult or even perhaps impossible to see. We needed to make that mental leap first.

Of course, it is true that problems cannot be regarded as being finally solved until solutions have been implemented and found to be effective. However we can now see, from the above discussion, that there are three main types of generic problem we need to be aware of:

- Problems of Definition
- Analysis Problems
- Lack of Insight Problems

The De Bono model is used for *creative* problem-solving, when we need to brainstorm imaginative solutions. The thinking required to do that is known as **divergent** thinking i.e. where we are looking for an array of possible solutions. Within a problem management context, the De Bono model can be particularly helpful when we are working on the production of **workarounds** (temporary solutions) because imagination is exactly what is required in that situation.

With regard to IT problems however, where we are looking for very specific *causes* that need to be identified and eradicated, a different type of thinking is required after the initial steps of **definition** and **analysis**. In this case, we are looking for a single, specific cause of [an] incident(s) and the thinking process we need to employ is actually the reverse of the above i.e. it is **convergent** thinking. To solve this type of problem, we need to use a much more analytical approach.

Kepner-Tregoe & Ishikawa

The ITIL® best practice framework recommends Kepner-Tregoe Problem Analysis for identifying the root causes of incidents. This problem analysis process is one of four processes defined within the Kepner-Tregoe Problem Solving and Decision Matrix (PSDM).

For completeness, here are the four Kepner-Tregoe processes in PSDM:

- Situation Appraisal ... clarify the situation

- Problem Analysis ... define problem and identify cause

- Decision Analysis ... alternatives and risk analysis

- Potential Problem Analysis .. alternatives scrutinised

The Kepner-Tregoe framework of processes can be applied to all types of problems (both within and outside of IT contexts, but they are considered best practice for structured critical thinking i.e. *analytical* problem-solving, as opposed to *creative* problem-solving. This was the actual methodology used on the Apollo 13 mission in which so many challenging problems were systematically defined and solved.

There are 5 steps to Kepner-Tregoe Problem Analysis:

- Define the Problem
- Describe the Problem
- Establish Possible Causes

- Test the Most Probable Cause
- Verify the True Cause

You will instantly notice some similarity with the Edward De Bono model that we looked at earlier. The first three steps are very similar indeed, but this analysis is much more focussed upon the identification of root-causes and it therefore goes into a different level of analysis with the 'Test' and 'Verification' steps.

Here is a description of the steps:

Define the Problem

When people call the Service Desk, their description of the issue they are reporting is often very poorly defined and can frequently be one of the main causes of delay in getting incidents efficiently resolved when Service Desk staff simply log the call exactly as it is reported. It is part of the responsibility of the Service Desk to question the user with a view to obtaining as clear a definition of the issue as possible and to do this effectively, they should be thinking in terms of *object* and *deviation*.

- Object: What is broken?

- Deviation: The difference between what it *should be* doing and what it *is* doing

As an example, when a user calls the Service Desk to report that 'my printer is printing garbage' effective questioning can reveal the *object* is an *HP 4000 Bubblejet printer* and the *deviation* is that the printer *is printing the top half of characters only*.

By just asking a few of the right questions, we see quite a difference in our problem definition:

- Printer is printing rubbish

- HP 4000 Bubblejet printer is printing the top half of characters only

That's much better! And Charles Kettering was absolutely right when he said that, "a problem well defined is a problem half solved."

Describe the Problem

This is the initial analysis step. It does not involve the application of logic (that comes later in this method) at this stage; it is simply an information gathering exercise that will be used when logic is applied during the later steps.

Suppose we had already **defined** the problem as: Microsoft Exchange Server Version XX, Service Pack YY, Patch Level ZZ intermittently reboots itself.

Here are the questions we need to ask in order to complete the problem description step ...

What?

What *IS* the system failure?
What *Other (similar) Systems* could have failed, but have *NOT*?
What is the *Difference*?
What has *Changed*?

Where?

> Where *IS* the failure location?
> Where have *Other (similar) Systems* that could have failed *NOT* done so?
> What is the *Difference*?
> What has *Changed*?

When?

> When *IS* the failure time(s)?
> When does the failure *NOT* occur?
> What is the *Difference*?
> What has *Changed*?

Extent?

> The *Number* of failed objects?
> The *Number* of other objects that could have failed, but *NOT* done so?
> What is the *Difference*?
> What has *Changed*?

It is helpful to represent your answers to those questions in a table. Below is a simple example of a completed table to give you the basic idea. Obviously, you would be much more verbose with your entries in practice.

	IS	Is NOT	Difference(s)	Change(s)
What?	Server	6 Others	None	All Patched
Where?	Sales Dept	Other Depts	Separate Buildg	Security
When?	Wed Eve	Other Days	Cleaning	Maint Company
Extent?	1	6	Tech Support	Outsourced

By answering the above questions, we have now discovered that the failed eMail Server is one of 7 identical servers (same manufacturer, hardware, operating system, service pack and patch level) that were recently patched. However, it is housed in a different building, it failed when the new maintenance company happened to be cleaning the building and the server that failed is externally supported i.e. technical support has been outsourced.

Representing the information in tabular format makes it much easier to analyse and identify possible causes which is the next step in the procedure.

Establish Possible Causes

It is now time to brainstorm the possible causes and if you have ever been involved in troubleshooting, you will already be very well aware that the cause of an IT problem is often due to some recent change(s). So our table now becomes very a useful tool in establishing possible causes.

For example, supposing that, during our brainstorming, we discovered that security in the separate building (where the sales department server is housed) had been recently changed. Could it be that there might be some security related access issue and as a result, we are dealing with an act of deliberate sabotage? It is certainly a possibility, so we want to include it on our list, no matter how unlikely we may deem it to be.

So now, using our table we can brainstorm a list of possible causes:

- Power Supply Issues

- External Support Company

- Cleaning (Maintenance) Company

- Security Issues

Ishikawa Diagrams

It can be very helpful to represent our possible causes using an Ishikawa diagram. Named after the originator (Kaoru Ishikawa) these diagrams are also commonly known as *fishbone* diagrams or *cause and effect* diagrams.

The idea is that, using a board or flipchart, the facilitator of a problem-solving group would draw a horizontal line and then write down the **effect** that we are investigating (usually on the right). Then, working from the Kepner-Tregoe analysis, as people identify and point out **possible causes**, the facilitator (usually the Problem Manager) would add branches that represent each of those possibilities.

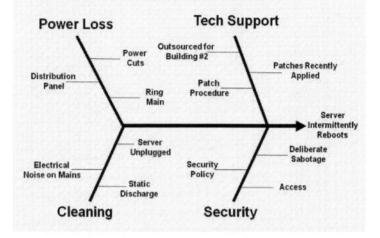

Fishbone Diagram (Ishikawa)

When the session is represented visually in this way, it can help to stimulate further discussion around each of the possible causes and sub-branches can be added to each of the main branches to represent the discussion.

Test the Most Probable Cause

The next step is to rank the possible causes in terms of likelihood so we can decide upon the *most probable cause*. So, as an example, taking four possible causes from the above Ishikawa diagram, here's how I would rank them using *High*, *Medium* or *Low* probability.

- External Support (who would have applied the recent patch) – **High**
- Power Supply Issues in Building #2 – **Medium**

- Unplugged Server to Plug-in Vacuum Cleaner – **Medium**

- Deliberate Sabotage – **Low**

We now need to *test* the most probable cause and the test question is: if _____ is the cause of this problem, does it explain what the problem *IS* and what the problem *COULD BE but IS NOT*?

My initial thoughts in ranking those possibilities were that the recently applied patch would have been applied by the external company, rather than our own internal support department, and that there could very well have been some procedural difference in the way the change was implemented. So, the answer to the test question above is that it certainly *could* explain why that particular server failed, and not the others.

Verify the True Cause

This is where logic comes into its own.

The final step is to go through all of the data in your table – remember that my table is deliberately brief (mainly because I wanted it to fit on a tiny Kindle screen) but your table will contain a lot more information in practice. So, if the ***most probable cause*** that you identified in the previous step is actually the ***true cause***, then it will fit with **ALL** of the observed data.

When you perform this level of analysis, you can see that my initial ranking was in fact faulty because the external support hypothesis does not explain why the incident occurs only on Wednesday evenings.

If the *most probable cause* does not map onto *all* of the observed data, then we need to pick one of the other *possible causes* (the next most likely from our initial ranking) and repeat the verification step i.e. check it against all of the data. Staying with our example, if the *new cleaning company* only cleans the building in which the server is housed and they only clean on Wednesday evenings, then we have now identified the *true cause* because, it fits with **ALL** of the observed data.

By the way, a number of years ago, in one of my own customer organisations, a cleaner was indeed found to be unplugging a server in order to plug-in a vacuum cleaner and was actually the cause of a similar issue.

Improving Your Logic

There is no question about it, you can definitely improve your ability to solve problems.

The average weight of a human brain is about three pounds and studies have, so far, estimated that it contains about 86 billion neurons (brain cells). These cells are arranged throughout the neo-cortex (the cauliflower part) of the brain to form a network through which electro-chemical signals are passed. No two brains are identical because, as you developed your intellect, you 'wired' your own brain.

Of course, we are here using the term 'wiring' simply as a metaphor but the wiring such as it is, consists of axons and dendrites – projections from the ends of the neurons - which physically grew within your brain. Your 'wiring' is what makes you very good at certain types of thinking. But you are not stuck with your current wiring which is very good news if you want to improve your ability to think logically and thereby become a better problem-solver.

The way you can improve your logical wiring is to engage in solving a series of problems that require logical analysis. We need to find problems that start at an easy level and then get progressively more difficult to solve. If you stick with this over a period of time, you will grow new connections and also strengthen some existing connections within your neural network and the result of this will be an improved ability to think logically.

Logic Grid Problems

The following problem is usually referred to as *Einstein's Logic Problem* and it is supposed to have been compiled in the 19th century. It is usually reported that Einstein said 98% of the people in the world would be unable solve it.

Now, there's a challenge for you ;)

Facts:

1: There are 5 houses in 5 different colours.
2: In each house lives a person of a different nationality.
3: These 5 owners drink a certain beverage, smoke a certain brand of cigar and keep a certain pet.
4: No owners have the same pet, smoke the same brand of cigar or drink the same drink.

With the following additional information, can you determine WHO KEEPS FISH?

1: The Brit lives in a red house.
2: The Swede keeps dogs as pets.
3: The Dane drinks tea.
4: The green house is on the left of the white house.
5: The green house owner drinks coffee.
6: The person who smokes Pall Mall rears birds.
7: The owner of the yellow house smokes Dunhill.
8: The man living in the house right in the centre drinks milk.
9: The Norwegian lives in the first house.
10: The man who smokes Blend lives next to the one who keeps cats.
11: The man who keeps horses lives next to the man who smokes Dunhill.

12: The owner who smokes Blue Master drinks beer.

13: The German smokes Prince.

14: The Norwegian lives next to the blue house.

15: The man who smokes Blend has a neighbour who drinks water.

The key to solving this problem is constructing a grid and once you have the grid worked out, solving it becomes quite mechanical. You can simply work through the clues and fill in details as you go and you should get the right answer.

	House 1	House 2	House 3	House 4	House 5
Country					
Colour					
Pet					
Beverage					
Cigarettes					

Sketch the above table on a piece of paper and see if you can fill it in from the statements in the problem. The right answer is shown below, so if you want to take a crack at it, do it before you read on.

By the way, it is unlikely that Einstein actually compiled this problem because of the anachronism relating to the type of cigar mentioned in the problem statement i.e. Blue Master cigars were not around during Einstein's life.

As you can see, with this type of problem, the real talent lies in the ability to construct the grid in the first place. Well here is the solution ...

	House 1	House 2	House 3	House 4	House 5

Country	Norwegian	Dane	Brit	German	Swede
Colour	Yellow	Blue	Red	Green	White
Pet	Cats	Horses	Birds	Fish	Dog
Beverage	Water	Tea	Milk	Coffee	Beer
Cigarettes	Dunhill	Blend	P/Mall	Prince	Blue M

Now, I wanted to begin this section by considering a logic grid type of problem to get them out of the way, so to speak. Because, as entertaining as they may be, I believe they have limited usefulness as far as improving our ability to think logically is concerned. They are not completely useless in this respect, but they are also not the best source of material for our purposes. The reason is quite simple: the types of problems we tend to encounter in life don't generally come along stated as neat little lists consisting of possible values.

So, what kind of analysis problems are best for our purposes? Here are some suggestions:

- Number Puzzles (Suduko™)
- Retrograde Chess Problems

Before we move on, it is important for you to understand that in learning to solve these particular analysis problems you are also learning to solve real problems. That is because of the *logic* step in both of the problem solving models we have discussed. We need to cultivate our ability to make accurate logical deductions and that's exactly what you will be doing when you work your way through these problems.

We'll now take a quick look at each of these approaches in turn.

Number Puzzles

The Number Puzzle is believed to have originated in the 18th century in Japan. It is a logic based puzzle known in the USA as *Number Place*. The puzzle is known as Sudoku™ in many other parts of the world. However that word is actually trademarked by the puzzle publisher (Nikoli Ltd) in Japan so herein we refer to the puzzle as the *Number Puzzle*.

Number Puzzles come in a variety of sizes. Most frequently the puzzles come in a 9 x 9 grid, which is made up of three 3 x 3 sub grids called regions. Some cells contain numbers called 'givens' or 'clues'. Your goal, as the player, is to fill in the empty cells. For a 9 x 9 puzzle, the rules are that each *cell* must contain only one number and each *row*, *column* and *region* must contain the numbers 1 to 9 just once.

There are simpler puzzles that use 4 by 4 grids with 2 x 2 regions and there are 6 by 6 grids with 2 x 3 regions and there are more difficult puzzles too. *The Times* publishes a challenging 12 x 12 grid with twelve 4 x 3 regions and you can find even bigger puzzles to challenge your thinking. 16 x 16 and even 25 by 25 grids have been published. So these puzzles perfectly fit with our criteria for improving your ability to think logically. You can get a Number Puzzle 'app' for your mobile phone too.

Below is a simple example using a 4 x 4 grid. The rules for a 4 x 4 grid are that each *cell* must contain only one number and each *row*, *column* and *region* must contain the numbers 1 to 4 just once.

See if you can solve it ...

4			1
	1	3	
	4	1	
1			3

By the way, don't worry about starting with the simplest puzzles. It's not where you start; it's where you finish that counts. You begin with simple puzzles to get your brain thinking in the right way and, at the same time, you will be beginning to rewire those important neural connections. Eventually, you will build up to the 9 x 9 puzzles and after that, there will be no stopping you!

Retrograde Chess Problems

When I went to school, it seemed that everybody could play chess; these days, that is no longer the case. However, my view is that it is worth learning how to play chess (if you can't) in order to have a go at these retrograde analysis problems. The first thing to note is that they are not like normal chess problems. That's because they are really logic problems using chess pieces.

The following problem, by Raymond Smullyan, is an excellent example to get you started on Retrograde Analysis.

Black moved last. What was Black's last move & what was White's?

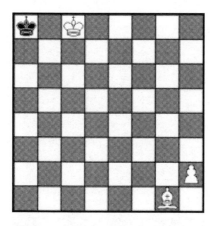

The pieces on the board are: *Black King*, *White King*, *White Bishop* and *White Pawn*. There are at least three possible answers to the problem and if you can find any of them, you are off to a great start.

Raymond Smullyan is a famous logician and his book *The Chess Mysteries of Sherlock Holmes* contains fifty of these retrograde analysis problems. The above problem is the simplest of them and they also get progressively more difficult as you move through the book, so again, they fit our criteria for improving our logical thinking ability perfectly.

Answers

With a bit of thought, I am sure you will have solved the above examples, but here are the solutions anyway.

Here is the solution to the Number Puzzle:

4	3	2	1
2	1	3	4
3	4	1	2
1	2	4	3

And here is the retrograde analysis solution:

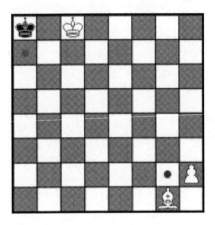

- Black moved the King from the square indicated by the red dot (top left) to get out of check.

- White moved a Pawn (no longer on the board) from the square indicated by the blue dot (bottom right) and promoted it to a Bishop.

You might think that is not a very good chess move, and that may or may not be true but the point is that the above solution fits the facts i.e. it is logically sound. Remember too that, as you learn to solve this kind of problem, you are simultaneously improving your ability to perform an accurate Kepner-Tregoe analysis.

As mentioned, there are at least two other possible solutions to the above chess problem. But think about them for yourself – it will do you good.

Improving Your Intuition

When we are told by psychologists that most of our thinking takes place at a subconscious level within the brain, we have every right to ask the question: how do they know? So, first, here is evidence that we do indeed think subconsciously: I am sure you will have experienced a situation in which you were chatting with another person and some specific question arose.

It was a question to which you knew the answer, but were simply unable to recall the information. Perhaps days passed and you had consciously 'forgotten' all about the conversation. Then, one day, when you were doing something completed unrelated and perhaps when you were totally relaxed – but certainly, long after you had stopped consciously trying to recall the information – the answer just popped into your conscious mind.

For me, I remember having a particular conversation about which actor had played the lead in *The African Queen* and it was days later, when I was doing the washing-up, when the subconscious mind dropped the answer – Humphrey Bogart - into my consciousness. When I tell this story in my workshops, the delegates will all nod their heads in agreement, no doubt recalling similar experiences. So I feel pretty sure that you will have had an experience like this too.

When you think about it, it is difficult to escape the conclusion that what happened was that you gave your mind a task to perform and, without your conscious knowledge, it got on with searching your memory banks (speaking metaphorically) until it found the requested information. This particular example is a very simple process i.e. memory retrieval. But it can come as a real surprise and a joy when you discover that your subconscious mind can solve problems too.

Here is an example from personal experience: there was one occasion when was trying to solve a particularly difficult intermittent IT problem. I was at a customer's site and I had been working on the problem all day. I had skipped lunch and was trying hard to resolve the issue before the end of the day because I needed to be at another site the following day. I continued to work on the problem long after all of the staff had left the building until, eventually, I was thrown out by the security staff. I thought I had tried everything but I was completely stumped.

Getting into my car, I started the drive home and selected some relaxing music. I was grateful to be 'off the case' so to speak, and I was enjoying the pleasant drive home through the countryside. Then, about half way home, the answer popped into my mind. It wasn't an idea - a thought that something might be the answer - it was the answer and I immediately knew it to be so. This was somewhat different to the memory retrieval experience because I certainly did not consciously know the answer before that moment and so the subconscious thinking that took place did actually involve solving the problem.

Since the above experience, I have practiced working with my subconscious mind and learning to trust in its remarkable abilities. When I am faced with any difficult decisions to make in life, I usually think about the situation in as much detail as I can, turning over the matter in my mind and then I simply live with it for a few days. During that time, I will take the dog for a long walk somewhere inspirational, usually along the beach or over the moors and during those walks I will try to *not* think about the matter at all. In fact, I will try to think of nothing but the walk and the view and how lucky I am to be living in such a beautiful place.

When I am living with a problem or 'walking with it' as a friend of mine once described the process, somewhere, usually within the period of a few days, I will know what to do. The right, or best possible, answer will simply formulate itself during that time. As John Steinbeck once said, "it is a common experience that a problem difficult at night is resolved in the morning after the committee of sleep has worked on it."

You have this amazing power of your subconscious at your disposal but you need to learn how to cultivate it and to trust in its abilities. It is a power that you can use for solving all kinds of problems, both within your work – whatever that happens to be - and also the wider problems you will naturally encounter in your life.

Here are some ways you can cultivate that ability:

- Meditation
- Yoga
- Tai Chi
- Walk the Dog
- Visualisation

What all of the above methods have in common is that they provide a way to quieten the conscious mind and this creates the space in which the subconscious can function most effectively. You need to find the method that works best for you, so try experimenting with the above methods until you find what you feel most 'at home' with and delivers the best results.

In closing this section, we should consider the proper place of intuitive thinking within problem-solving. Intuition enables us to find solutions to problems that require us to think creatively, not analytically. Remember that intuition has no place in a logical analysis. Logic is all about hard facts: *yes* and *no*, *right* and *wrong*, *ones* and *zeros*, *true* and *false*. It is not about *gut feelings* and *hunches* – but that is the province of intuition. Remember though, that you can certainly combine logic and intuition, by logically testing your intuitive ideas and suggestions.

Aside from the many diverse problems that life throws at us during our sojourn here, remember that intuition can also help us to solve problems within an IT context when creativity is required. Most notably, within the context of Problem Management, the generation of *workarounds* (temporary fixes) often requires this type of creative thinking.

Pareto & Pain Value Analysis

Vilfredo Pareto was an Italian economist and philosopher who became most famous for what has become known as the *80/20 Law* (also known as *Pareto's Principle*).

Essentially, this principle says that in many diverse fields of endeavour, about 80% of the *effects* will be produced by only 20% of the *causes*. Just from that brief introductory statement, as far as problem-solving is concerned, we can immediately see some relevance; especially so within an IT context where we have problems *defined* as causes.

The principle was derived from observation. Now, of course, we do need to be careful about generalising from observations (induction) – remember the *all swans are white* mistake made by early European explorers? That's why I personally like to think of it as a *principle* rather than a *law*. That said, this principle has been found to hold remarkably true in so many widely differing situations.

Pareto's first observation was that, in Italy during his time, roughly 80% of the land was owned by only 20% of the population. He thought this fact was interesting and when he began looking at wealth distribution in other countries, he found that the same ratio tended to hold true. He later noticed that, in his garden, about 20% of the pea pods contained 80% of the peas.

Since then, applying the principle to business situations, studies have revealed that in many organisations:

- About 80% the sales come from roughly 20% of the customers

- About 80% of the output is produced by around 20% of the staff

- About 20% of process defects are responsible for about 80% of the issues

As far as we can tell, from observation, it is a correct principle. In fact, if I am ever asked to guess a percentage, my reasoning always goes like this:

- Will the number be high or low? (usually an easy estimate)

- If I think the number will be high, I always guess 80%

- If I think the number will be low, I always guess 20%

And guess what? I am right about 80% of the time ;)

So, within a problem management context, how is this principle used?

Quite simply, it is used as a method of prioritising the problems that are waiting to be dealt with. Essentially, Pareto tells us that 80% of all of the incidents (effects) we are currently logging will be produced by just 20% of the problems (causes). So, if we can identify that 20% - separating the *critical few* from the *trivial many* – and deal with them first - then we have a very effective strategy for extracting the maximum benefit from our efforts.

Pain Value Analysis (PVA)

Pain Value Analysis is a method of assessing the *impact* (the effect on the organisation) of incidents and problems. Essentially, your organisation would need to agree upon a formula for calculating this pain and the following factors are often taken into account in such formulas:

- Number of incidents caused by a problem

- Average duration of an incident

- Average severity of an incident (No of people affected)

Here is an example of a PVA formula for assessing the **pain value** of problems:

Pain Value = (No. of Caused Incidents) x (Average Duration) x (Severity)

But it is only an example. In practice, you would use whatever metrics you think are appropriate and right for your organisation. Here are some more possible factors you could take into account when constructing your own formula:

- How much downtime?
- What is the cost to the business?
- How many services are affected?
- Are any VBFs affected?

N.B. In ITIL® jargon, a mission-critical element of the business is known as a VBF (Vital Business Function).

Using Pareto & PVA Together

There are various tools that can help you to rank problems by their *pain value* and then mathematically calculate the 20% of problems you should be focussing upon based on Pareto's Principle. But it is all very straightforward.

As an example, consider the following list of complaints that a hotel chain has received:

Reception Staff	19
Check-in	130
Breakfast	10
Restaurant	46
Telephones	1
Lifts	5
Night Service	6
Laundry	2
Room Service	10
Bar	1
Total Complaints	**230**

The complaint category is shown on the left and the number of complaints received last month, for each category, is on the right. For this example, we will use a very simple PVA formula and simply consider the *pain value* to be equal to the number of complaints received for each category.

Adding up all of the complaints, the total is 230 for the month, so:

80% of 230 = 184

Now we need to identify the categories that together constitute 80% of the complaints i.e. the sum of which is nominally equal to 184.

From the table, we can easily see that by attending to the *Reception Staff*, the *Check-in* and the *Restaurant* issues, you would be addressing just over 80% (i.e. 195) of the total complaints received in the month. If you were to only attend to the top two, you would be addressing just under 80% (i.e. 177) of the complaints.

Working with a list of incidents and their **pain values**, you could derive similar conclusions using a simple spreadsheet. You would sort the incidents by *pain value* and then arithmetically select the top 20% that are causing 80% of the headache (pain).

However, in practice, it really is very simple because in a list of 10 items, Pareto is telling us that about 20% of that list (i.e. 2 items) will be responsible for about 80% of the pain.

As long as you don't allow the desire for mathematical precision to get in the way, you could very quickly and easily decide which two items on the list you should prioritise. There would be no need for graphs or calculations in our example: it is obvious which two causes you should be addressing first (*Check-in* and *Restaurant*) and, if you were to crunch the numbers, you would find that those two issues actually account for 76.96% of the complains received – see, that's about 80% of the headache (unless you are an accountant).

With a longer list, you can do exactly the same kind of thing. Simply rank the items in descending order, by *pain value*, and then choose the top 20% to focus on first – easy! It does not mean, of course, that you can ignore the other things on your list. Remember that Pareto Analysis is simply a method of prioritising.

Proximal, Distal & Root-Causes

Let's return to the story of Apollo 13 and the explosion that caused so many incidents that it thwarted the mission and almost cost the lives of the crew.

Let's look again at the reported incidents and the underlying problem:

Incidents reported by the Apollo 13 crew:

- There was a sharp bang and vibration
- There is a main B bus undervolt
- We have lost two of our three fuel cells
- One [oxygen] tank appears to be completely empty
- The second [oxygen] tank is rapidly being depleted

Problem: an under-rated thermostatic switch in the in the oxygen tank's circuitry that caused an explosion.

From the above, you can quite easily see that there was actually more than one cause i.e. the incidents were directly caused by the explosion but the explosion had another cause – the thermostatic switch. The immediate cause is technically known as the **proximal cause** and the deeper cause is technically known as the **distal cause**. So, in this example, the **proximal cause** (immediate cause) of the incidents was the explosion and the **distal cause** (the *cause* of the cause) was the under-rated switch.

But we could go even further. By continuing to question 'why something occurred' we can get down to **root-causes**, sometimes referred to as *ultimate causes*. So let's continue to work with this example and now consider the following question:

Why was the thermostatic switch in the oxygen tank circuitry under-rated? Well, here is another extract from Jim Lovell's account of the mission:

In case you are wondering about the cause of it all, I refer you to the report of the Apollo 13 Review Board, issued after an intensive investigation. In 1965 the Command Module had undergone many improvements, which included raising the permissible voltage to the heaters in the oxygen tanks from 28 to 65 volts DC. Unfortunately, the thermostatic switches on these heaters weren't modified to suit the change.

- *Jim Lovell, Captain Apollo 13*
http://history.nasa.gov/SP-350/ch-13-1.html

From the above report, we can see that the answer turns out to be that a failure of the *change management* process at NASA had occurred. It was, in fact, a failure to properly assess the impact of raising the permissible voltage to the oxygen tank heaters – and this is considered to be the **root-cause** of the accident.

The scenario provides a very good example and illustration of why many organisation's problem management processes are not as effective as they might be.

Supposing that the investigation into the explosion had ended with the identification of the under-rated switch – after all it was the cause of the explosion. If that were the case, then the corrective action might involve checking all remaining Saturn 5 rockets and replacing the identified component and it might also involve changing specifications so that Saturn 5 rockets are not built in the future with that under-rated component in the infrastructure.

If the above action were initiated, you might think that problem management had done a pretty good job. But, if we were to not also address the issue of the faulty change management process, who knows what other incorrect impact assessments might ensue and what the consequences might have turned out to be for future missions.

Just one last thing before we move on: having identified that the change management process was at fault, should we go even further and ask the question, 'why was the change management process faulty?' It could be that the database used for impact assessments - the Configuration Management Database (CMDB) in ITIL® - was inaccurate. Now, if that turned out to be true, might we then go even further and ask ourselves, 'why was the CMDB not up-to-date?'

Of course, we *can* go on and if it serves the goals of the organisation to go deeper, then it is indeed sensible to do so. If you keep asking the 'why' question, at some stage, you will reach a point where it is clear that the **root-case** has been found.

The 5 Whys Technique

It is generally considered that five iterations of asking the 'why' question will be enough to identify a *root-cause*, hence the name of this technique which was developed by Sakichi Toyoda in the 1930s.

Here's a simple example:

Q: **Why** did the car stop?
A: Because it ran out of petrol.

Q: **Why** did it run out of petrol?
A: Because the warning light did not illuminate.

Q: **Why** did the warning light not come on?
A: Because a fuse had blown.

Q: **Why** had the fuse blown?
A: Because of an electrical short-circuit.

You may reach the root-cause at any stage and, in the above example, there is no need to go further than the 4th iteration because the electrical short-circuit is the *root-cause* so we can stop there. Always bear in mind that the technique is most effective when those people who have direct, hands-on experience of the process being examined are actually answering the questions.

When dealing with complex processes and systems, there may be many different possible answers to any particular 'why' question and therefore this technique is not suitable for every problem. So it is worth adding here that when we *are* dealing with complex systems, it can be very helpful to perform a *Chronological Analysis* of the sequence of events. Once an accurate timeline of events has been constructed and is available to problem-resolver groups, it can be a lot more straight-forward to understand which event triggered the next. Using such a timeline, we can then work backwards to identify the root-cause.

There are three basic types of cause to be aware of:

- Physical Causes ... Tangible items failed

- Human Causes ... People did something wrong

- Organisational Causes ... A system, process, or policy is faulty

In identifying a root-cause, just as in our Apollo 13 example where the change management process was found to be faulty, you are typically looking for a *process* or a *behaviour* that can be introduced or changed so, when you find that, you can stop and then get on with initiating the necessary corrective action.

Problem Management Process

Now let's take a look at the ITIL® process for Problem Management. The aims of the process include preventing incidents from happening, eliminating recurring incidents and reducing the impact of incidents that cannot be prevented, which it does by defining and documenting temporary measures known as *workarounds*.

Workarounds are one of two main outputs of the process; the other is permanent *resolutions*. Workarounds are recorded in the KEDB (Known Error Database) for future reference and resolutions are initiated via RFC (Request for Change) and then progressed by the Change Management process.

Here is an example Problem Management process; you would have as many or as few steps as appropriate for your organisation ...

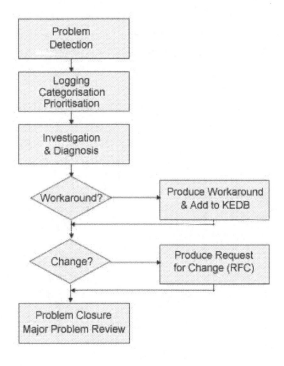

Here is a description of the individual steps:

Detection – is identification that a problem exists

Logging – involves recording the problem in a database

Categorisation – generally uses the same categories as Incident Management

Prioritisation – involves setting an initial priority

Investigation & Diagnosis – is finding the root-cause

Workaround – producing a temporary fix

Resolution (Change) – initiating corrective action

Closure – formally closing the problem record

Major Problem Review – is a lessons learned exercise

Now, let's look at those steps in more detail …

The process is kicked-off with the identification that a problem exists (*detection*) and we have already discussed most of the methods. However, to our list, we should add the automatic detection of problems by our Event Management tools. An **event** is not an incident; it is a 'change of state' that has some significance for us as a service provider. To illustrate, supposing you were driving along and the petrol warning light illuminated on your car dashboard (because we have now had it fixed, of course).

Everything is working fine: we are still driving and there is no interruption to normal operation. However, if we do nothing about that warning, we are going to finish up with an interruption (incident). The *change of state*, in this example, is that the fuel level has dropped below a threshold that we are monitoring – it is a very good example of an event. Not all events are warnings; some events occur as part of the normal operation of our systems, for example, a user logging in is an event.

In many organisations, the event management process is automated so we typically have tools deployed in the infrastructure that are capable of detecting these changes of state, working out their level of significance and then initiating the appropriate control action – whatever that needs to be. That action could be to raise an incident in order to get a human being involved; it could be to trigger some automated response, for example, to run a prepared script; it might be to raise an RFC (Request for Change). These automated responses are usually programmed into our event management toolset.

So we can also program those same tools to raise a problem record if a certain set of conditions is met. For example, bearing in mind that the event management tools are capable of automatically raising incidents, if an incident is found to be recurring, we can quite easily program the same tools to automatically raise a problem record. So our list of detection methods now looks like this:

- Repeating incidents
- Information made available by another party
- Multiple simultaneous incidents
- Trend Analysis using incident data
- Automated detection

The *logging* step involves raising a record in the problem database, one of the many databases in the CMS (Configuration Management System) in ITIL®. Generally, modern service management toolsets have the ability to link problem records to related incidents. The problem record will be used to document the progress of the problem from initial detection through to final closure.

The purpose of *categorisation* is to determine what is affected. Within our toolset, at the top level, there will probably be a broad hardware/software division and within each of those top-level categories there will be sub-categories. For example, within the software category, there may be various applications. The important thing is that this activity will use the same categories and codes as the incident management process.

In the *prioritisation* step, the *impact* (effect on the organisation) and *urgency* (target time to fix) of related incidents needs to be assessed, as well as the severity of the problem itself. Assessing severity essentially involves applying the organisation's formula for determining *pain value* and the problem manager will be well aware that a Pareto Analysis on incidents ranked by pain value is very effective method of prioritising problems.

Investigation and Diagnosis involves using the array of problem-solving tools and techniques we have, hitherto, been discussing - Kepner-Tregoe, Ishikawa Diagrams, the 5 Whys Technique, Chronological Analysis, Pain Value Analysis and Pareto Analysis - to identify underlying causes (both proximal and distal) and to arrive at root-causes.

As mentioned, the main outputs of the process are *workarounds* (temporary measures) and permanent *resolutions* i.e. corrective action initiated by RFC (Request for Change). The process might produce either of these, or both – in some cases, where the cost of a permanent solution is high and the inconvenience of living with the problem is relatively low, the organisation may decide not to progress the permanent fix.

Workarounds are documented on the problem record within our Problem Database and recorded in the KEDB (Known Error Database) – both of these databases reside within the CMS (Configuration Management System) in ITIL ®. The idea of the KEDB is that should an incident recur, the Service Desk can often immediately identify and apply a workaround thereby reducing the impact of the incident.

It is worth mentioning Knowledge Management at this stage i.e. "getting the right information to the right person at the right time" in order to facilitate the right decision. Good IT Service Management toolsets will have some kind of knowledge management facility built-in and the KEDB (Known Error Database) that is populated and maintained by the problem management process will be an important component of it.

The following diagram shows the basic structure of the Service Knowledge Management System (SKMS) ...

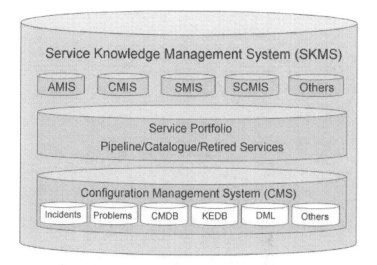

You can see from the above that the CMS is but one of many Management Information Systems (MIS) within the SKMS. Inside the CMS are various databases including not only the CMDB and KEDB, but also the Incident and Problem Databases where incident and problem records are stored.

When corrective action has been taken and found to be effective, the problem record can be closed (*closure*) along with any related incidents that may still be open. At this point, the problem manager would ensure that the problem record is fully up-to-date with the historical details of the problem and details of the corrective action that has been successfully applied.

Following a major problem, the problem manager would conduct a *lessons-learned* exercise (*major problem review*) in order to educate staff and incorporate those lessons into our working methods, for example, diagnostic scripts might be updated as a result. In addition, the actions from the review meeting will be fed to the Service Level Manager for subsequent reporting to the customer.

As the great William Edwards Deming (no relation) once said, "Learning is not compulsory ... neither is survival."

Ensuring that we are 'learning and growing' as an organisation is not only an important way of maintaining good customer relationships, it is also one of the criteria that any successful business will usually require to be demonstrated over time. For that reason, it is often one of the four perspectives used on a *Balanced Scorecard* – a top level reporting method used by many organisations. So 'lessons learned' both from the major problem review and many other similar reviews performed by other service management processes can provide useful metrics that are aggregated to provide that assurance.

Introducing

The design of a process is one of the responsibilities of the *Process Owner* role. A role is simply a collection of responsibilities and it is perfectly possible for an individual to occupy more than one role. In ITIL® there is a distinction between *Process Owner* and *Process Manager* roles but it is not uncommon for these to be combined.

Here are the responsibilities of each:

Process Owner

The *Process Owner* has overall accountability for the process, ensuring the process is both 'fit for purpose' and 'fit for use'. The process is said to be 'fit for purpose' if it does what it should do and it is 'fit for use' if it consistent and can be depended upon.

It is the *Process Owner* role that is concerned with ensuring the process works as intended, that it complies with appropriate policies and that it delivers value to the business. Any process failures are escalated to the *Process Owner* so that the process can be reviewed and changed if necessary to prevent similar failures in the future.

Specific responsibilities include:

- Advocacy/Sponsorship
- Overall Design
- Ensuring Value
- Policy Compliance

- Defining CSFs
- Defining KPIs
- Process Integration
- Managing Process Failures
- Continual Improvement

Critical Success Factors (CSF) are things you need to have in place in order for the process to have a good chance of success. For example, a CSF for *Problem Management* would be to have an effective *Incident Management* process in place. Many of the CSFs for Problem Management relate to the ability of these two processes to properly interface and interact.

Key Performance Indicators (KPI) are important metrics that provide the Process Owner and Manager roles with proper visibility of the effectiveness of the process. For example, the 'percentage of problems that resulted in SLA (Service Level Agreement) breaches' would be a good KPI for Problem Management. Clearly this figure should be reducing if we were getting better at Problem Management.

Process Manager

The *Process Manager* is a much more hands-on (operational) role and is involved in planning, managing and coordination of the day to day execution of the process. There may be a number of *Process Managers* for different areas of responsibility all working within the same process. For example, you might have different *Change Managers* each with responsibility for a separate geographical region.

The specific activities of the *Process Manager* will actually be defined by the *Process Owner* who is responsible for overall design of the process including specifying roles and responsibilities. However, these responsibilities will typically include:

- Planning and Coordination
- Checking Inputs/Outputs
- Guiding Practitioners
- Monitoring and Reporting

The Problem Manager

So the responsibilities of the *Problem Manager* role, in many organisations, amounts to a combination of the above activities i.e. the responsibilities of both *Process Owner* and *Process Manager*. Typically the person filling this role will need to have a certain amount of organisational authority to ensure the execution, and improvement of the *Problem Management* process receives proper attention and investment.

Introducing Problem Management

The ITIL® recommendation for the introduction of *Service Operation*, i.e. the entire Lifecycle Phase within which *Problem Management* sits, is to consider running it as a project.

Here are The ITIL® *Service Operation* processes:

- Incident Management ... Deals With Service Disruptions

- Problem Management ... Identifies and Removes Underlying Causes

- Request Fulfilment ... Handles User Requests that are not Service Disruptions

- Access Management ... Grants and Revokes Rights and Privileges

- Event Management ... Detects and Handles Changes of State that are not Service Disruptions

Of course, much of *Service Operation* is likely to already exist within any organisation looking to introduce the *Problem Management* discipline. So, the *CSI (Continual Service Improvement) Approach,* which is shown below, is a useful way of thinking about how the project might be scoped and managed at a top level.

The CSI Approach:

- What's the Vision?
- Where are we Now?
- Where do we Want to Be?
- How do we Get There?
- How do we know we've Arrived?
- How do we keep the Momentum Going?

The *vision* might be the one provided by ITIL® i.e. to have an effective and mature *Service Operation* capability with all five processes nicely integrated and in place. In order to get there, we need to create and implement our plan i.e. to run our project. The 'where are we now' and 'where do we want to be' questions from the above approach are very useful in helping to determine the starting point (our baseline) and a measureable target for the project.

Baselining could be done on a process-by-process basis i.e. by first considering which of the five *Service Operation* processes the organisation already has in place. The important idea with this approach is to understand that you need not get the whole thing implemented in a single step i.e. you can go around that little cycle in a number of steps, introducing new processes and improvements with each successive iteration.

In addition, it is helpful to understand that processes are rarely optimal when they are first introduced. They usually reach maturity over time and after successive improvement initiatives have been introduced. So bear in mind that you probably won't get things absolutely right first time. However, as long as you build in improvement mechanisms i.e. ensure that the process is properly owned and managed, you will ultimately reach your goal of having a mature *Problem Management* process in place.

In Closing

Whether you were looking to improve your analytical skills, improve your knowledge of ITIL® or simply learn more about the subject of problem management, I hope you have found something of value in this book.

Like me, you may be the kind of person who just loves to solve problems. If so, remember that problem-solving is not just for fun and it's not something to be reserved for the workplace; it is a life-skill ... in fact, it is the key life-skill because it is the way you can accomplish pretty much anything you set your heart on achieving.

When facing any seemingly daunting problem, always bear in mind the tremendous power of the tools and techniques we have been considering within this book. Remember too, that shifting your perspective is often a very important prerequisite to accessing the best solutions.

In his biography of Steve Jobs, Walter Isaacson reports the recollections of Tony Fadell, one of the leading designers on the Apple iPod project:

"There would be times when we'd rack our brains on a user interface problem, and think we'd considered every option, and he [Steve Jobs] would go, 'Did you think of this?' ... And then we'd all go, 'Holy Cow!' He'd redefine the problem or approach, and our little problem would simply go away."

Finally, remember that there is always a solution for every problem ... even if, at first, you just can't see it.

About the Author

William A Edwards is a graduate of the University of Birmingham, England. He began his career in IT in 1973 and was Technical Manager of Apricot International during its heyday.

He holds the ITIL® Expert certification and is a lifetime member of the British Computing Society. These days, he writes books, blogs about his passions and still runs the occasional ITIL® training workshop.

If you have found this book helpful, I would be very grateful if you would leave a review at the bookstore where you purchased it.

Thank you,

Will Edwards

William A Edwards MBCS

Glossary

In compiling the glossary, a number of difficult decisions were made regarding which definitions to include and exclude. This scoping activity needed to be done because the official ITIL® site manages a huge glossary of terms. It is believed that the following list of terms, whilst not exhaustive, should be very useful to the reader.

Architecture

(*ITIL Service Design*) The structure of a system or IT service, including the relationships of components to each other and to the environment they are in.

Asset

(*ITIL Service Strategy*) Any resource or capability. The assets of a service provider include anything that could contribute to the delivery of a service.

Availability

(*ITIL Service Design*) Ability of an IT service or other configuration item to perform its agreed function when required.

Baseline

(*ITIL Continual Service Improvement*) (*ITIL Service Transition*) A snapshot that is used as a reference point.

Best Practice

Proven activities or processes that have been successfully used by multiple organizations. ITIL® is an example of best practice.

Business Case

(*ITIL Service Strategy*) Justification for a significant item of expenditure. The business case includes information about costs, benefits, options, issues, risks and possible problems.

Business Process

A process that is owned and carried out by the business. A business process contributes to the delivery of a product or service to a business customer.

Business Unit

(*ITIL Service Strategy*) A segment of the business that has its own plans, metrics, income and costs. Each business unit owns assets and uses these to create value for customers in the form of goods and services.

Capability

(ITIL Service Strategy) The ability of an organization, person, process, application, IT service or other configuration item to carry out an activity. Capabilities are intangible assets of an organization.

Change

(ITIL Service Transition) The addition, modification or removal of anything that could have an effect on IT services. The scope should include changes to all architectures, processes, tools, metrics and documentation, as well as changes to IT services and other configuration items.

Change Advisory Board (CAB)

(ITIL Service Transition) A group of people that support the assessment, prioritization, authorization and scheduling of changes.

Change Proposal

(ITIL Service Strategy) (ITIL Service Transition) A document that includes a high level description of a potential service introduction or significant change, along with a corresponding business case and an expected implementation schedule.

Change Schedule

(ITIL Service Transition) A document that lists all authorized changes and their planned implementation dates, as well as the estimated dates of longer-term changes.

Change Window

(ITIL Service Transition) A regular, agreed time when changes or releases may be implemented with minimal impact on services. Change windows are usually documented in service level agreements.

Charter

(ITIL Service Strategy) A document that contains details of a new service, a significant change or other significant project. Charters are typically authorized by service portfolio management or by a project management office.

Configuration Item (CI)

(ITIL Service Transition) Any component or other service asset that needs to be managed in order to deliver an IT service. Information about each configuration item is recorded in a configuration record within the configuration management system (CMS) and is maintained throughout its lifecycle by service asset and
configuration management.

Configuration Management System (CMS)

(ITIL Service Transition) A set of tools, data and information that is used to support service asset and configuration management. The CMS is part of an overall service knowledge management system and includes tools for collecting, storing, managing, updating, analysing and presenting data about all configuration items and their relationships.

Critical Success Factor (CSF)

Something that must happen if an IT service, process, plan, project or other activity is to succeed. Key performance indicators are used to measure the achievement of each critical success factor.

CSI Register

(ITIL Continual Service Improvement) A database or structured document used to record and manage improvement opportunities throughout their lifecycle.

Definitive Media Library (DML)

(ITIL Service Transition) One or more locations in which the definitive and authorized versions of all software configuration items are securely stored. The definitive media library may also contain associated configuration items such as licences and documentation.

Emergency Change Advisory Board (ECAB)

(ITIL Service Transition) A subgroup of the change advisory board that makes decisions about emergency changes. Membership may be decided at the time a meeting is called, and depends on the nature of the emergency change.

Event

(ITIL Service Operation) A change of state that has significance for the management of an IT service or other configuration item. The term is also used to mean an alert or notification created by any IT service, configuration item or monitoring tool. Events typically require IT operations personnel to take actions, and often lead to incidents being logged.

Function

A team or group of people and the tools or other resources they use to carry out one or more processes or activities – for example, the service desk.

Governance

Ensures that policies and strategy are actually implemented, and that required processes are correctly followed. Governance includes defining roles and responsibilities, measuring and reporting, and taking
actions to resolve any issues identified.

Impact

(ITIL Service Operation) (ITIL Service Transition) A measure of the effect of an incident, problem or change on business processes. Impact is often based on how service levels will be affected. Impact and urgency are used to assign priority.

Incident

(ITIL Service Operation) An unplanned interruption to an IT service or reduction in the quality of an IT service. Failure of a configuration item that has not yet affected service is also an incident – for example, failure of one disk from a mirror set.

IT Service

A service provided by an IT service provider. An IT service is made up of a combination of information technology, people and processes. A customer-facing IT service directly supports the business processes of one or more customers and its service level targets should be defined in a service level agreement.

IT Service Management (ITSM)

The implementation and management of quality IT services that meet the needs of the business. IT service management is performed by IT service providers through an appropriate mix of people, process and information technology.

IT Service Provider

(ITIL Service Strategy) A service provider that provides IT services to internal or external customers.

IT Steering Group (ISG)

(ITIL Service Design) (ITIL Service Strategy) A formal group that is responsible for ensuring that business and IT service provider strategies and plans are closely aligned. An IT steering group includes senior representatives from the business and the IT service provider.

Key Performance Indicator (KPI)

(ITIL Continual Service Improvement) (ITIL Service Design) A metric that is used to help manage an IT service, process, plan, project or other activity. Key performance indicators are used to measure the achievement of critical success factors.

Known Error

(ITIL Service Operation) A problem that has a documented root cause and a workaround. Known errors are created and managed throughout their lifecycle by problem management. Known errors may also be identified by development or suppliers.

Known Error Database (KEDB)

(ITIL Service Operation) A database containing all known error records. This database is created by problem management and used by incident and problem management. The known error database may be part of the configuration management system, or may be stored elsewhere in the service knowledge management system.

Major Incident

(ITIL Service Operation) The highest category of impact for an incident. A major incident results in significant disruption to the business.

Metric

(ITIL Continual Service Improvement) Something that is measured and reported to help manage a process, IT service or activity.

Monitoring

(ITIL Service Operation) Repeated observation of a configuration item, IT service or process to detect events and to ensure that the current status is known.

Operational Level Agreement (OLA)

(ITIL Continual Service Improvement) (ITIL Service Design) An agreement between an IT service provider and another part of the same organization. It supports the IT service provider's delivery of IT services to customers and defines the goods or services to be provided and the responsibilities of both parties.

Outsourcing

(ITIL Service Strategy) Using an external service provider to manage IT services.

Problem

(ITIL Service Operation) A cause of one or more incidents. The cause is not usually known at the time a problem record is created, and the problem management process is responsible for further investigation.

Process

A structured set of activities designed to accomplish a specific objective. A process takes one or more defined inputs and turns them into defined outputs. It may include any of the roles, responsibilities, tools and management controls required to reliably deliver the outputs. A process may define policies, standards, guidelines, activities and work instructions if they are needed.

Release

(ITIL Service Transition) One or more changes to an IT service that are built, tested and deployed together. A single release may include changes to hardware, software, documentation, processes and other components.

Release Package

(ITIL Service Transition) A set of configuration items that will be built, tested and deployed together as a single release. Each release package will usually include one or more release units.

Release Unit

(ITIL Service Transition) Components of an IT service that are normally released together. A release unit typically includes sufficient components to perform a useful function.

Reliability

(ITIL Continual Service Improvement) (ITIL Service Design) A measure of how long an IT service or other configuration item can perform its agreed function without interruption. Usually measured as MTBF or MTBSI. The term can also be used to state how likely it is that a process, function etc. will deliver its required outputs.

Remediation

(ITIL Service Transition) Actions taken to recover after a failed change or release. Remediation may include back-out, invocation of service continuity plans, or other actions designed to enable the business process to continue.

Request for Change (RFC)

(ITIL Service Transition) A formal proposal for a change to be made. It includes details of the proposed change, and may be recorded on paper or electronically. The term is often misused to mean a change record, or the change itself.

Resource

(ITIL Service Strategy) A generic term that includes IT infrastructure, people, money or anything else that might help to deliver an IT service. Resources are considered to be assets of an organization.

Risk

A possible event that could cause harm or loss, or affect the ability to achieve objectives

Role

A set of responsibilities, activities and authorities assigned to a person or team. A role is defined in a process or function. One person or team may have multiple roles – for example, the roles of configuration
manager and change manager may be carried out by a single person.

Service

A means of delivering value to customers by facilitating outcomes customers want to achieve without the ownership of specific costs and risks. The term 'service' is sometimes used as a synonym for core service, IT service or service package.

Service Acceptance Criteria (SAC)

(ITIL Service Transition) A set of criteria used to ensure that an IT service meets its functionality and quality requirements and that the IT service provider is ready to operate the new IT service when it has been deployed.

Service Catalogue

(ITIL Service Design) (ITIL Service Strategy) A database or structured document with information about all live IT services, including those available for deployment. The service catalogue is part of the service.

Service Design Package (SDP)

(ITIL Service Design) Document(s) defining all aspects of an IT service and its requirements through each stage of its lifecycle. A service design package is produced for each new IT service, major change or IT service retirement.

Service Improvement Plan (SIP)

(ITIL Continual Service Improvement) A formal plan to implement improvements to a process or IT service.

Service Knowledge Management System (SKMS)

(ITIL Service Transition) A set of tools and databases that is used to manage knowledge, information and data.

Service Level Agreement (SLA)

(ITIL Continual Service Improvement) (ITIL Service Design) An agreement between an IT service provider and a customer. A service level agreement describes the IT service, documents service level targets, and specifies the responsibilities of the IT service provider and the customer. A single agreement may cover multiple IT services or multiple customers.

Service Lifecycle

An approach to IT service management that emphasizes the importance of coordination and control across the various functions, processes and systems necessary to manage the full lifecycle of IT services. The service lifecycle approach considers the strategy, design, transition, operation and continual improvement of IT services.

Service Management

A set of specialized organizational capabilities for providing value to customers in the form of services.

Service Portfolio

(ITIL Service Strategy) The complete set of services that is managed by a service provider. The service portfolio is used to manage the entire lifecycle of all services, and includes three categories: service pipeline (proposed or in development), service catalogue (live or available for deployment), and retired services.

Service Provider

(ITIL Service Strategy) An organization supplying services to one or more internal customers or external customers. Service provider is often used as an abbreviation for IT service provider.

Service Request

(ITIL Service Operation) A formal request from a user for something to be provided – for example, a request for information or advice; to reset a password; or to install a workstation for a new user. Service requests are managed by the request fulfilment process, usually in conjunction with the service desk. Service requests may be linked to a request for change as part of fulfilling the request.

Serviceability

(ITIL Continual Service Improvement) (ITIL Service Design) The ability of a third-party supplier to meet the terms of its contract. This contract will include agreed levels of reliability, maintainability and availability for a configuration item.

Stakeholder

A person who has an interest in an organization, project, IT service etc. Stakeholders may be interested in the activities, targets, resources or deliverables. Stakeholders may include customers, partners, employees, shareholders, owners etc.

Statement of Requirements (SOR)

(ITIL Service Design) A document containing all requirements for a product purchase, or a new or changed IT service.

Supplier

(ITIL Service Design) (ITIL Service Strategy) A third party responsible for supplying goods or services that are required to deliver IT services. Examples of suppliers include commodity hardware and software vendors, network and telecom providers, and outsourcing organizations.

Supporting Service

(ITIL Service Design) An IT service that is not directly used by the business, but is required by the IT service provider to deliver customer-facing services (for example, a directory service or a backup service).

Test Environment

(ITIL Service Transition) A controlled environment used to test configuration items, releases, IT services, processes etc.

Underpinning Contract (UC)

(ITIL Service Design) A contract between an IT service provider and a third party. The third party provides goods or services that support delivery of an IT service to a customer. The underpinning contract defines targets and responsibilities that are required to meet agreed service level targets in one or more service level agreements.

Urgency

(ITIL Service Design) (ITIL Service Transition) A measure of how long it will be until an incident, problem or change has a significant impact on the business. For example, a high-impact incident may have low urgency if the impact will not affect the business until the end of the financial year. Impact and urgency are used to assign priority.

Utility

(ITIL Service Strategy) The functionality offered by a product or service to meet a particular need. Utility can

be summarized as 'what the service does', and can be used to determine whether a service is able to meet its required outcomes, or is 'fit for purpose'. The business value of an IT service is created by the combination of utility and warranty.

Value on Investment (VOI)

(ITIL Continual Service Improvement) A measurement of the expected benefit of an investment. Value on investment considers both financial and intangible benefits.

Vital Business Function (VBF)

(ITIL Service Design) Part of a business process that is critical to the success of the business. Vital business functions are an important consideration of business continuity management, IT service continuity management and availability management.

Warranty

(ITIL Service Strategy) Assurance that a product or service will meet agreed requirements. This may be a formal agreement such as a service level agreement or contract, or it may be a marketing message or brand image. Warranty refers to the ability of a service to be available when needed, to provide the required capacity, and to provide the required reliability in terms of continuity and security.

Workaround

(ITIL Service Operation) Reducing or eliminating the impact of an incident or problem for which a full resolution is not yet available – for example, by restarting a failed configuration item. Workarounds for problems are documented in known error records. Workarounds for incidents that do not have associated problem records are documented in the incident record.